101 Questions and Answers on the Prophets of Israel

101 QUESTIONS AND ANSWERS ON THE PROPHETS OF ISRAEL

Victor H. Matthews

Paulist Press
New York/Mahwah, NJ

Cover design by Cindy Dunne

Library of Congress Cataloging-in-Publication Data

Matthews, Victor Harold.
    101 questions and answers on the prophets of Israel / Victor H. Matthews.
        p. cm.
    Includes bibliographical references.
    ISBN 978-0-8091-4478-5 (alk. paper)
    1. Bible. O.T. Prophets—Criticism, interpretation, etc. 2. Prophets. I. Title.
    BS1505.52.M38 2007
    224′.061—dc22

                                                            2007006249

Published by Paulist Press
997 Macarthur Boulevard
Mahwah, New Jersey 07430

www.paulistpress.com

Printed and bound in the
United States of America

CONTENTS

INTRODUCTION

Like the other volumes in the "101 Questions and Answers" series, this book is designed to serve as a useful companion to a portion of the biblical text. In this case, the focus is on prophets and prophecy, and this book briefly explores commonly asked questions and provides nontechnical answers designed to assist laypeople, ministers, and students with the world and words of the prophets of ancient Israel. I begin with a few introductory answers that provide an introduction to the basic character of prophecy in the ancient Near East and how it compares to that found in the Bible. The remainder of the volume deals with various prophetic figures, some not always associated with prophecy (Abraham), who appear throughout the biblical narrative.

The survey begins with those narratives that deal with the emergence of the Israelites as a distinct people and examines those individuals (Moses, Balaam, Samuel) who set a tone or established precedents for later prophetic speech and action. During this early period I will often be examining a biblical narrative outside the traditional books assigned to the prophets and addressing a question such as "Why do the seventy elders prophesy in Numbers 11:24–30?" Once I move into the period of the monarchy, attention will be given to how the prophets are closely tied to events in the history of Israel. In fact much of what I will have to say about them will reflect the changing fortunes of the nation: from the formation of the united monarchy to the division of the kingdoms, and the disasters of the eighth and sixth centuries when Israel and Judah were caught between the political ambitions of Egypt and the Mesopotamian empires of Assyria and Babylonia. In every case, however, we will discover that the influences or threats from other nations are perceived by the prophets as part of God's control over events and in particular as divine responses to the people's obedience or disobedience to the stipulations of the covenant.

Since my own interests center on the social world of ancient Israel, I have often chosen to examine aspects of the story that require a closer look at such things as historical geography, sacred space, or comparative religion. For example, the answer to the question, "Why is Elijah's battle against the prophets of Baal on Mt. Carmel so critical?" will touch on the Mediterranean climate, the revival of a cultic site, and the theme of the "contest between gods." In other cases, I will provide basic information to assist the reader on aspects of cultural background or social world details, such as "Why should a foreigner who worships other gods consult a prophet of Yahweh? (1 Kgs 5)." In this particular narrative, the political situation (war between Syria and Israel) serves as the background, but the focus is on a man afflicted with leprosy who consults a prophet in order to obtain a cure.

There is a great deal to learn about everyday life in ancient Israel in the references to farming and commerce in the prophets. For instance, when I answer "What makes the Song of the Vineyard in Isaiah 5 such a powerful oracle?" I will deal with the backbreaking labor involved in building hillside terraces and the patience that must go into cultivating a vineyard for years before it becomes productive. In a similar vein, in my answer to the question, "Why are the New Moon and the Sabbath so important for Amos's judgment on Israel? (Amos 8:4–6)," it is possible to glimpse the tensions created by religious restrictions on commerce.

In addressing the smaller, lesser-known prophetic books, I have chosen to provide brief summaries of their basic themes. I hope this will spark greater interest in exploring how they fit both into the prophetic corpus and into the history of ancient Israel. For the major prophets, I have provided several entries that step through the prophet's message, methods of delivery, and historical setting. In some cases this will deal with a particularly significant event, such as the siege of Jerusalem in 701 BCE by the Assyrian king Sennacherib. Or, I have focused on an effective prophetic metaphor (Hosea's marriage) or method of delivery (Jeremiah's letter to the exiles in Babylon or Ezekiel's "street theater" performances). Rounding out the collection are questions on different types of prophecy, including ecstatic and apocalyptic. Charts have been embedded into the text to provide quick overviews of themes or point to comparisons between the prophets.

In every case, the answers are designed to aid the layperson, minister, or religious professional to more quickly gain a basic understanding of the biblical world and the role of the prophets. I have tried to avoid technical language where possible; when this was impossible, because there are simply some terms that are necessary to biblical studies, I have provided definitions or explanations. It is my hope that this book will be used in a variety of educational settings. It is basic enough to be used in Bible study groups or church school settings. Plus it contains enough information that it could serve as a supplementary textbook in Bible as Literature classes, Introduction to Hebrew Bible courses, or Introduction to the Prophets classes in university or seminary settings. Wherever it is used, by an individual or a group, I hope that it will spark further study and bring the importance of the biblical prophets into even sharper focus.

Victor H. Matthews
Missouri State University
Springfield, Missouri
August 2006

ONE

INTRODUCTORY QUESTIONS

1. What are the prophetic books in the Bible?

A significant portion of the canon of Hebrew Scriptures is made up of the named books of the prophets, comprising sixteen of the thirty-nine recognized as authoritative. Since such a large proportion of the Bible is dedicated to prophecy it is clear that it was an extremely important vehicle for expressing God's word in ancient Israel. In addition to the prophets found in these books, there also are many prophets, both named and unnamed, who are mentioned in the biblical narratives but who do not have their own books. Most of these figures date to the early period of Israel's monarchy (Nathan, Elijah, Elisha) or are only briefly mentioned in the narrative (Gad, Micaiah, Huldah). The prophetic books in the Christian canon begin with Isaiah, Jeremiah, and Ezekiel, the three longest books of prophecy. This is followed by a collection of twelve Minor Prophets, plus the Book of Daniel, which contains apocalyptic visions and is therefore considered by some to be a book of prophecy as well. If they had been arranged in chronological order rather than by size and relative importance, the collection would begin with Amos and end with Daniel. Some also contain more than one section representing different time periods. The central themes in all of the prophetic books are (1) a call to return to obedience to the covenant, (2) warnings that disobedience will spark divine displeasure and punishment, and (3) that the righteous remnant will repent and therefore survive God's expression of anger to rebuild and restore the nation. The books consist of historical narrative, prophetic oracles or pronouncements, and accounts of events in the lives of the prophets. Unlike the books from Joshua through Kings (often referred to as the Former Prophets), the books of the Latter Prophets do not always follow a logical sequence of events. Instead many of them are simply collections, in no particular order, of sermons, prophetic speeches, and enacted dramatizations of oracles.

2. What is the difference between the "early" and "later" prophets?

The history of ancient Israel spans several centuries and the activities of the prophets are most evident during the period of the monarchy (ca. 1000–586 BCE). It is therefore to be expected that the social and historical context of the chronologically "early" prophets and the "later" prophets would be quite different even if the core message (obedience to the covenant) remains the same. The concerns of the nations, both economic and political, drove events, created crises, and necessitated periodic reminders that the hope for the people must be based in their belief in Yahweh. Despite the time-based differences and challenges, there are some common themes found in all of the prophetic literature. These include (1) concern over the abuse of power manifested in the activities of the kings (see Gad's confronting David over a census in 2 Sam 24:11–14) and the priestly community (see Ezekiel's complaint against "false shepherds" in Ezek 34:1–10); (2) the contest between Yahweh's supporters and the advocates of other gods (see Elijah on Mt. Carmel in 1 Kgs 18); and (3) championing the rights of the poor (Elisha restores a lost ax head in 2 Kgs 6:1–7; Amos condemns the indulgent women of Samaria in Amos 4:1–4). Many of the prophets express their concerns in "divine lawsuits" that have God standing in the court and calling upon all to witness the unfaithfulness of the people (see Micah 1:1–7 and Isa 5:1–7). However, because prophets often spoke about specific events in their own time there are variations on the major prophetic themes. For instance, Nahum speaks at a point just before the destruction of the hated Assyrian empire about 615 BCE. His emphasis is entirely on how these Mesopotamian dynasts are at last receiving just recompense for the horrible crimes they had committed against Israel and other nations. This stands in contrast to prophets with broader, more elaborate messages like Ezekiel, who does speak of immediate things like the immanent destruction of Jerusalem in 587 BCE, but who also sketches out in some detail the future return of the people to rebuild the Temple and restore the nation.

3. What is the nature of a prophetic call or vocation?

Prophets are called to their vocation by God. They can be men or women, young or old, well connected or peasant farmers. They all, however, share the experience of being called to serve as God's voice to the people, and they all speak on a common theme: obedience to the covenant. While there are some spectacular accounts of a prophet's call, such as Moses's experience on Mt. Sinai or Isaiah's vision of God's presence in the Jerusalem Temple, the biblical narrative does not always provide a detailed account of each prophet's initial contact with God. Some, like Amos, simply state that they were "called" from their everyday existence to go and speak, while others contain no account whatsoever. In those instances where an elaborate call narrative does appear in the text, certain commonalities are present: (1) a theophany or appearance of the deity to the human occurs, (2) an attempt is made on the part of the human to avoid the call, giving excuses why he or she is unworthy or ill-equipped for the task, (3) an act by the deity empowers the person being called and sets aside their excuses, and (4) a statement of mission is provided providing some scope to their task and directing them to begin. It should also be noted that the prophetic vocation can last a lifetime, as is the case with Jeremiah, or it may be limited to a brief period and a specific goal, as in the case of Jonah's mission to warn the people of Nineveh. In every case, however, they speak in the name of the deity and their words or actions are to be considered part of the divine message rather than a personal statement.

4. Are there different types of prophets in Israelite society?

Ancient Israel, like its neighbors, recognized that prophetic speech could be and was voiced by religious professionals as well as by common people. Even so, there were two principal types of prophets in ancient Israel. The court prophet functions as a diviner, whose task is to determine the future through external means (e.g., interpretation of cloud formations, the entrails of sheep, or by casting of lots) or by interpreting dreams or visions sent from God. Since they work directly for the palace, these prophets are sometimes suspected of only speaking what their employer wishes to hear (see Jehoshaphat's question in 1 Kgs 22:7). This is not to say that all court prophets are bound in loyalty to their king and cannot or will not speak God's message. Nathan, for instance, clearly is a part of David's court and one of his advisors. This does not, however, prevent Nathan from confronting the king when he committed adultery with Bathsheba (2 Sam 12:1–15), or advising David when he believes the king is in danger of making a mistake on the royal succession (1 Kgs 1:22–27). Independent prophets, who may, like Isaiah, actually be members of the professional priesthood, function primarily as champions of the covenant with God. This often brings them into conflict with authority figures like the priests and kings. It is their task to stand up to all forms of pressure, whether it be verbal abuse (Amos 7:12–13) or physical intimidation (Jer 20:2) and state without reservation the message they have been given by God. The seriousness of their task is found in the "sentinel" image in Ezekiel 3:17–21 in which the prophet is warned that he must speak, even in the face of the people's rejection of his message, or their blood will be on his hands.

5. Do the prophets speak mainly during times of crisis?

The role of the prophet in ancient Israel was to serve as a champion of the principles of the covenant: obedience to God's word, compassion and care for every member of the covenant community, and a passion for justice in society. As a result, there is no one instance in which the prophets speak, although some of the most spectacular examples of prophetic speech do come during times of extreme national crisis. Thus we find David's court prophet Nathan describing how God does not require the building of a temple in Jerusalem, but will instead create a "house" or dynasty for David's line of rulers (2 Sam 7:4–17). In another instance, an unnamed prophet from Judah confronts King Jeroboam during a dedication ceremony at Bethel. This could be described as a crisis of practice since Jeroboam intends to establish a competing form of worship in Bethel that does not conform to that in Jerusalem. Anticipating a future time of trouble for Israel, Amos comes to Bethel while that nation is experiencing a period of peace and prosperity. His harsh message contrasts with current conditions, but does employ typical prophetic speech reminding the people that their contentment is predicated on God's goodwill. Their failure to care for all of the people, including the poor and the weak, constitutes a gross violation of their obligation to the covenant community and to God. Crisis is, of course, a time for prophetic activity. For example, Isaiah confronts King Ahaz as he prepares to face an invasion of Judah by a coalition lead by Israel and Syria (Isa 7:3–9), and Jeremiah calls on the people to surrender to the besieging Babylonians and to accept this as God's judgment on the nation (Jer 21:1–10). However, by the time the nations of Judah and Israel are in such dire straits, there is little that the prophets can say other than that the people must accept their responsibility for the calamitous events and see the coming punishment as God's justice (a process known as theodicy—the rationalization of why God allows events to occur). In these cases, the prophet's traditional role as an intercessor for the people, praying on their behalf to God (see Gen 20:7; Deut 9:22–29), is set aside and they are explicitly told by God not to pray for the people (Jer 7:16). It then becomes the responsibility of the prophets to speak for the benefit of the remnant who will hear and respond to the call to repent. The crisis is only a manifestation of covenant breaking and the message is designed to ensure that there will be a future for the nation.

6. What were the various types of biblical prophecy?

The stereotypical image of a biblical prophet is a person standing in the street before a crowd and crying out a message in the name of God. There are examples of this type of behavior, but this is a simplistic way of portraying a prophet's activities. Prophecy can take place anywhere. Although most prophetic speech is oral, it is often complemented by gesture and pantomime, and some prophetic speech occurs in front of a private audience (a king or priest) or is shaped as a soliloquy by the prophet assisting current events and describing events that are in the far future. To be systematic about this, however, it can be said that biblical prophecy takes the form of (1) ecstatic speech and movement, (2) public sermons, (3) street theater involving unlikely actions and unusual props by the prophet, and (4) visionary or eschatological pronouncements that generally do not require an audience. Ecstatic speech and movement involves the loss of physical control of the body as a result of a frenzy brought on by a drug or the emotions generated by music and/or dance. It results in a trance-like state and utterances that may have to be interpreted by a diviner or priest. This type of prophecy is found throughout the ancient Near East with references that include the Egyptian *Tale of Wenamon* (eleventh century BCE) and the Mari Letters from upper Mesopotamia (eighteenth century BCE). Biblical examples are found in Saul's joining the prophetic frenzy of a band of men playing instruments (1 Sam 10:5–6, 10–11) and Elisha's request for a musician before being infused with the "power of the Lord" (2 Kgs 3:15). Public sermons include a conscious decision about where to stage the message and contain detailed statements about current events that need to be brought to the attention of the people (i.e., Jeremiah's standing before the gate of the Jerusalem Temple). These sermons are often anchored by references to earlier examples of divine intervention (exodus event, military victories, or destruction of earlier cultic sites) and thus are designed to evoke responses from the audience that are lost on modern readers. Street theater or pantomime performances are examples of enacted prophecies that combine speech with dramatization such as Ezekiel's play acting with an inscribed, "besieged" brick that is intended to evoke alarm and questions about Jerusalem's fate (Ezek 4:1–3). Finally, the recital and interpretation of dreams and visions is not limited to apocalyptic or eschatological prophecy (see Micaiah in 1 Kgs 22:19–23), but they are more common in later works like Zechariah 9–14 and Daniel 7–12.

7. Were there prophets in other ancient Near Eastern countries?

There is textual evidence that prophets and prophecy existed in other ancient Near Eastern cultures. The existing sources, however, have some surprising gaps. For instance, there are no examples found at the Syria seaport city of Ugarit, and the only Hittite text mentioning prophets is the fourteenth-century BCE *Plague Prayers of Mursilis*. In this text, the king calls on the gods to declare their purpose in bringing calamity on the people by sending dreams or the declaration of a prophet. Some differences in the texts also may be cultural. In Egypt where the pharaoh is considered to be a god, the only direct reference to possession by a god and the resulting ecstatic pronouncement is found in the eleventh-century *Tale of Wenamon*. Most of what exists from Egypt appears in the form of literary productions such as the *Visions of Neferti* (eighteenth century BCE) or the *Admonitions of Ipuwer* (twelfth century BCE). They provide predictions, but in a wisdom context where a sage makes formal statements without referring to a specific god. This stands in contrast to the much richer corpus of prophetic texts found in Mesopotamia. The administrative letters from Mari mention at least three groups of male and female prophets who provide the king with advice and warnings. The *āpilum* prophets spoke for specific state gods or collectively for the will of the divine assembly of all the gods. The *assinu* prophets were genderless temple personnel and their pronouncements represented the word of a god from a specific sanctuary and generally involved rituals or sacrifices, and the *muḫḫû* prophets were ecstatics, whose message came spontaneously or in trance state and often involved cultic matters or the word of a god/goddess to whom they were devoted. The personal names of the prophets never appear in the Mari letters, which could indicate that they were considered members of a sacred social class of persons whose names could not be spoken. In the Neo-Assyrian sources (ca. 900–600 BCE), ecstatic prophets are referred to as *raggimu*, and their oracles were actually collected and placed into archives by the Assyrian kings.

8. What is the difference between priests and prophets?

Although both priests and prophets operate within a religious context and serve God in various capacities, there are some fundamental differences between these two groups. Priests must be male members of the tribe of Levi and high priests must be descended from Aaron. As portrayed in the Holiness Code in Leviticus, they are concerned with the correct performance of sacred rituals and the maintenance of ritual purity. Prophets are divine messengers who can be either gender and from any of the tribes, and their primary task is to call the people back into compliance with the covenant. Thus, the often-repeated statement by prophets that "it is better to obey than sacrifice" (1 Sam 15:22) sums up their attitude toward the relative importance of temple construction and maintenance, animal sacrifice and national festivals, and other forms of ritual in comparison to obedience to the tenets of the covenant. Confrontation does occur between priests and prophets over their right to speak for God or to supersede the importance of temple activities. For example, when Jeremiah publicly curses the city of Jerusalem and its houses and palaces in a ritual of execration, he is arrested by Pashur, the "chief officer in the house of Lord," and placed in the stocks in an attempt to discredit his prophetic message (Jer 19:1–20:2). While not directly confronting a specific priest in his denunciation, Hosea collectively refers to them as a band of robbers and murderers, who have lead Israel into idolatry and failed to recognize that what God desires is "steadfast love and not sacrifice" (Hos 6:6–9). This is not to say that the entire priesthood of ancient Israel was corrupt or was obsessed with the mechanical aspects of religious practice. Priests did serve an important role in gathering the tithes and redistributing surplus grain or other commodities from the temple treasuries. They maintained the religious calendar, adjudicated disputes, and investigated suspicious deaths and contaminated persons and property. All of these tasks were important to the religious life of the nation. Prophets, however, were not tied to particular shrines or to the strictures of ritual. They had a simpler, even more basic role as social critics and the voice of conscience protecting the rights of the poor and the weak, and reminding the powerful that the only true authority came from God.

9. What was the relationship between prophets and kings?

It is an interesting thing that the two positions in ancient Israel that are described as being commissioned directly by God are the prophet and the king. Potentially, they had complementary roles in assisting the people, but instead they are generally portrayed in the biblical narrative as either adversaries or rivals. Of course, prophets were also the instrument used by God to anoint and thus designate a person as king or king-to-be. Both Saul and David are anointed by Samuel (1 Sam 9:15–10:8; 16:1–13), the prophet Ahijah indicates to Jeroboam that he will become king of Israel by giving him ten pieces of a robe (1 Kgs 11:26–32), and Elisha sends a member of his prophetic community to the Israelite general Jehu to anoint him, initiating a civil war (2 Kgs 9:1–10).

In each of these scenes, the civil authority is subsidiary to the representative of God. Although these kings owed a measure of their authority to the actions of the prophet, it must have been a source of contention between them as well. This is made quite clear in the repeated disputes between Samuel and Saul (1 Sam 13–15) over their individual prerogatives and powers as God's designated representatives. When the kingdom divided and Jeroboam took several political and religious steps to create a separate identity for the northern kingdom of Israel (see 1 Kgs 12:25–33), the prophets are particularly active in condemning "Jeroboam's sin" and the kings who continued these scandalous practices. Amos sarcastically calls on Israel to "come to Bethel (one of Jeroboam's designated shrines) and transgress" (4:4), while Hosea calls into question the legitimacy of the Israelite kings, saying "they made kings, but not through me" (8:4). King Ahab practically whines over having to consult a prophet outside his own court circle, telling his fellow king Jehoshaphat "there is still one other…but I hate him, for he never prophecies anything favorable about me" (1 Kgs 22:8). Kings found themselves in the unenviable position of having to go to the prophets for advice or to obtain word of God's intention for the nation. For instance, in the midst of the siege of Jerusalem in 587 BCE, King Zedekiah sends his advisors to Jeremiah to "inquire of the Lord on our behalf" hoping that the response will be that "the Lord will perform a wonderful deed for us" (Jer 21:2). Their "hat-in-hand" petition only made them look even more pitiful when the prophet proclaimed God's decision not to spare the city but instead to "fight against you with outstretched hand and mighty arm" (Jer 21:5). Being free of political considerations, prophets could call on a king to sit quietly and allow the divine warrior to bring victory or salvation to the nation (see Isa 7:3–4; Jer 27:12–15). Few leaders had the courage to stand up to this type of challenge. As a result, there are only a few instances in the biblical narrative in which a king combines consultation with a prophet and abject supplication to God in prayer for the nation (see Hezekiah's actions in 2 Kgs 19:1–34).

10. What is a basic chronology of the prophets within the history of ancient Israel?

Not all of the prophets mentioned in the biblical text play a significant role in shaping the history of the nation. In addition, there is some uncertainty about whether some of the earliest of these individuals should be described as a prophet or whether they simply possess some of the attributes of prophets while playing a broader role as leader of the people. Listed below are the major time periods of Israelite history (approximate dates indicate a lack of clear evidence) and a list of associated prophetic figures with a brief synopsis of their significance.

ca. 1800–1500 BCE   Ancestral Period

Abraham—founder of the nation; introduces Yahweh worship in the Promised Land (Gen 12–23)

ca. 1250–1150 BCE   Exodus and Wilderness Period

Moses—leads the exodus from Egypt, transmits the Decalogue to the people prior to their conquest of Canaan (Exod 3–20, 24, 32)

Balaam—foreign prophet; demonstrates the universality of Yahweh's power (Num 22–24)

ca. 1150–1000 BCE   Settlement Period

Deborah—female judge who predicts an Israelite victory (Judg 4–5)

Samuel—functions as judge, priest, and prophet; anoints first two kings (Saul and David) in 1 Samuel 1–16

ca. 1000–900 BCE   Early Monarchy Period

Nathan—David's court prophet; pronounces the everlasting covenant and confronts the king over his adultery with Bathsheba (2 Sam 7:1–17; 12)

Ahijah—designates Jeroboam first king of divided kingdom (1 Kgs 11–12, 14)

Unnamed Prophet of Judah—condemns Jeroboam's shrine at Bethel (1 Kgs 13)

ca. 900–721 BCE   Divided Monarchy Period

Elijah—ninth-century miracle worker; wins contest on Mt. Carmel, condemns Ahab for stealing Naboth's vineyard (1 Kgs 17–2 Kgs 2)

Elisha—ninth-century miracle worker; rewards the sons of the prophets, heals Na'aman, chooses Jehu to remove the House of Ahab (2 Kgs 2–9)

Micaiah—ninth-century prophet who stands up to royal and rival prophetic pressures to describe a dream theophany and Ahab's demise (1 Kgs 22)

Amos—early eighth-century farmer from Tekoa who goes to Bethel to condemn improper worship and social injustice

Hosea—late eighth-century Israelite; warns of the impending Assyrian crisis and uses a marriage metaphor to signal that God is still willing to take the nation back if they repent their idolatry

721–586 BCE   Late Monarchy Period

Isaiah—the first section (chaps. 1–39) late eighth-century prophet; challenges Ahaz and Hezekiah to trust Yahweh in the face of the Assyrian threat

Micah—a rural prophetic voice during the Assyrian invasion in the late eighth century; condemns Samaria and Jerusalem for political and religious arrogance, calls for a simpler understanding of the covenant

Nahum—late seventh-century prophetic voice who rejoices over the destruction of the Assyrian capital of Nineveh as a sign of God's judgment on the nations

Zephaniah—active during reign of Josiah (640–609 BCE), known for oracles against the nations standing as a warning to Jerusalem to reform, and an apocalyptic eschatology in which the purified nations recognize Yahweh's power

Jeremiah—active between 625–586 BCE, delivers message of impending destruction of Jerusalem and the beginning of the exile

Huldah—late seventh-century female prophet; authenticates the "Book of the Law" for King Josiah (2 Kgs 22:14–20)

Habakkuk—late seventh-century prophet; message includes a dialogue between the prophet and God, a series of woe oracles, and a psalm

Ezekiel—called in 595 BCE while in exile, warns of the destruction of Jerusalem (587 BCE), and points to a restoration after the purification of the exile

586–535 BCE   Exilic Period

Second Isaiah—speaking ca. 540 BCE, this portion of Isaiah (chapters 40–55) attempts to create a theodicy for the exile in four "Servant Songs" and calls on the exiles to return to Jerusalem

535–400 BCE   Postexilic Period

Haggai—single issue prophet of the 520s; lobbies governor Zerubbabel to take up the mantle of Davidic leadership and rebuild the Jerusalem Temple

Zechariah—chapters 1–8 (late sixth century BCE), contains a series of apocalyptic visions centering on the need to rebuild the Jerusalem Temple

Third Isaiah—speaking after the rebuilding of the Jerusalem Temple ca. 515 BCE (chaps. 56–66), contains an inclusive message emphasizing Sabbath

Jonah—set in Assyrian period (eighth century), actually dates to postexilic period, uses worst-case scenario to promote the universalism theme

Joel—postexilic temple official (ca. 500 BCE), message contains an emphasis on the "Day of Yahweh," an ecological crisis in the form of a locust plague

Malachi—mid- to late-fifth century, condemns the lack of devotion by the Jerusalem priesthood, mixed marriages, divorce, and failure to pay tithes

Deutero-Zechariah—chapters 9–14 (fifth century BCE), emphasis on end-time events including a final battle in which Yahweh emerges triumphant

ca. 325–150 BCE   Hellenistic Period

Daniel—set in the exile, composed in the early second century BCE, contains wisdom stories, dream interpretation and apocalyptic visions reflecting developments in Judaism down to the time of the Maccabean Revolt

Prophets in the Pentateuch

11. Is Abraham a prophet? (Gen 20)

Abraham is only referred to as a prophet in a single text (Gen 20:7). In this second example of the motif of Wife-Sister Deception (see Gen 12:10–20), Abimelech, king of Gerar, takes Sarah into his harem, unaware that the ancestral couple has tricked him. The king is warned by God in a dream to return Sarah to her husband or face his own death and that of his people. If he complies, Abraham the prophet (Hebrew: *nābî*) will pray for him and God will then spare his life. Apparently, Abimelech was familiar with the abilities of prophets and does not delay in complying. In this narrative, as in the bargaining session recounted in Genesis 18:16–33 to spare the potentially righteous persons of Sodom, Abraham functions as an intercessor. This prophetic role is also found in the accounts of Moses (Num 11:2; Deut 9:20), Samuel (1 Sam 7:8–9), and Elisha (2 Kgs 4:33). Portraying Abraham as a prophet adds greater authority to the founder of the nation (compare the political value attached to Saul's spontaneous prophetic speech in 1 Sam 10:10–13). It is also a certification of Abraham's worthiness as the first to receive the covenant promise despite the fact that nothing is said about his character prior to God's speaking to him.

12. Is Moses a prophet?

Moses operates simultaneously as a sage and law-giver, a priest, a civil administrator, and an intercessory prophet. Thus, the response to this question is that Moses was indeed a prophet, but he was also much more. Several precedents are established during the course of his career that will serve as models for prophetic speech and behavior:

Mosaic Prophetic Precedents			
Call Narrative	Moses (Exod 3–4:17)	Isaiah (Isa 6)	Jeremiah (Jer 1:4–18)
Contest between Gods Motif	Plagues (Exod 7–12)	Elijah on Mt. Carmel (1 Kgs 18)	Daniel interprets Nebuchadnezzar's dreams (Dan 2, 4)
Intercessory Prayer	Wilderness Period Murmuring (Num 11:1–3; 14:13–19)	Samuel (1 Sam 7:8–9; 12:19; Jer 15:1)	Elisha (2 Kgs 4:33)

Dialogue with God	Moses's complaint (Num 11:10–15)	Jeremiah's complaint (Jer 20:7–18)	Habakkuk's complaint (Hab 1)
Confrontation with Authority Figures	Korah's revolt (Num 16:1–35)	Amos's reply to Amaziah (Amos 7:11)	Jeremiah's trial (Jer 26:7–19)
Impact as Prophet on the Nation	Moses's obituary (Deut 34:10–12)	Samuel's Farewell Address (1 Sam 12)	Elijah's ascent and return (2 Kgs 2:11; Mal 4:5)

Not surprisingly, later writings (see Ps 106:23) and prophetic figures drew on Moses's authority either by making reference to his significant deeds (see Isa 63:11–12) or matching elements of their career to his. Thus Elijah, like Moses, spends time in the wilderness before finding his way to Mt. Horeb (= Mt. Sinai) to receive a call to further service by God (1 Kgs 19:4–18). Both Isaiah and Jeremiah seek to make excuses, like Moses, when confronted by God's call, and both of them, like Moses (Exod 4:10–16), are empowered to speak despite their complaint that they cannot (Isa 6:5–7; Jer 1:6–9). Moses's ability to speak freely to God, even raising complaints about the burdens of leadership (see Num 11:10–15), sets a precedent that is followed by Jeremiah in his cry that God has "enticed" him, allowed him to become a "laughing-stock" and forced him to speak an unpopular message (Jer 20:7–18). The compassionate role of the prophet as intercessor for the people is demonstrated repeatedly during the wilderness trek when Moses has to step in to save the disobedient or grumbling people from God's wrath (see Num 11:1–3; 14:13–19; 16:41–50). Moses's courage in facing conflict situations such as his strong response to Korah's revolt (Num 16:1–35) is a fitting model for Jeremiah's unflinching defense of his prophetic mission in his trial before the Jerusalem authorities (see Jer 26:7–19). Finally, the full impact of Moses's authority on later generations is even found in his obituary, which asserts that "never since has there arisen a prophet in Israel like Moses" (Deut 34:10).

13. Why do the seventy elders prophesy in Numbers 11:24–30?

One of the realities of leadership that Moses had to learn was that he could not cope with all of the situations that arose in the Israelite encampment in the wilderness. Based on the advice of his father-in-law, Jethro, Moses had previously appointed judges who could share the judicial burden to adjudicating the major and minor disputes among the people (Exod 18:13–26). Now after leaving Mt. Sinai and beginning their trek through the wilderness, Moses came to realize that he also needed to share the position as God's spirit-filled leader for the people. They had come to expect him to be able to fulfill their every need and he was so affected by this that he called on God to kill him and put him out of his misery (Num 11:14–15). The solution comes when God commands Moses to gather the seventy elders of the people, the men who have already been recognized as leaders by their tribes (see Exod 24:1–11). Once they are standing in company before the Tent of Meeting where God's presence is manifested among them, God takes a portion of the divine spirit that had been invested in Moses and places it in each of the seventy elders (compare Balaam in Num 24:2). As a result, they are overcome by the power of the spirit (like Saul in 1 Sam 10:5, 10–11) and they all engage in a form of ecstatic prophecy. In this way, the people knew that a portion of God's power was placed in their leaders and they could rely on them, as they did upon Moses, for advice and for the solution to their problems. One difference, however, between the elders and Moses is that unlike Moses, after they had prophesied, "they did not do so again" (Num 11:25).

14. Why does the foreign prophet Balaam speak in the name of Yahweh? (Numbers 22–24)

Balaam is the only non-Israelite prophet who is mentioned in both the biblical text and in an extrabiblical inscription found at Deir 'Alla in the Jordan valley. In this inscription Balaam has a dream that the gods plan to destroy his city by ordering Shagar, the god of light, to lock the gates of heaven, obscuring the sun. In the resulting darkness a topsy-turvy world is created (a theme also found in the Egyptian *Visions of Neferti*). One signal of this is that all the animals become confused and reverse their natural roles. Fearing that his dream will come true, Balaam goes into mourning. When the people ask him why he is downcast, he tells them about the dream so that they will repent, and call on the divine assembly to spare the city. Several of the elements of this story are also found in prophetic narratives in the Bible. For example, the prophet Micaiah has a dream in which Yahweh's divine assembly has gathered and a decision is made to deceive King Ahab so he will be killed in battle (1 Kgs 22:19–22). The motif of a darkened world with nature turned upside down also is found in Joel 2:10. Given these similarities it makes a great deal of sense for a well-known prophet to be brought into an Israelite story to demonstrate the power of Yahweh to command and control even those known to have a reputation as a conduit for divine speech. Just as God uses Cyrus the Persian king to free the exiles from Babylonian captivity even though the king is unaware of being directed to do so (Isa 45:1–6), in this narrative in Numbers God employs Balaam to make the point that true prophets speak for Yahweh.

Two

Early Monarchy Period

15. How does the Deuteronomistic Historian portray the prophets and prophecy?

In the long history of compiling and editing the materials that eventually found their way into the canonical form of the Hebrew Scriptures, several individuals and groups contributed narratives, genealogies, poetry, royal annals, wisdom sayings, prophetic oracles, and songs. One group, whose final composition of a coherent account of the Israelite monarchic period most likely occurred in the early sixth century BCE, has been identified by scholars as the author(s) of the Deuteronomistic History, referred to as the Deuteronomistic Historian. Their work is seen in the books of Deuteronomy through Second Kings. Characteristics that distinguish their editorial style and their religious and political agenda include:

Characteristics of the Deuteronomistic Historian

a "southern perspective," which emphasizes the unquestioned role of Jerusalem as the place where God caused his name to dwell (Deut 12:5; 1 Kgs 8:29) and the need to centralize worship around the Jerusalem Temple (see Hezekiah's reform in 2 Kgs 18:3–6 and Josiah's reform in 2 Kgs 23:1–27)

an emphasis on the legitimacy of the Davidic monarchy in Judah (see the "everlasting covenant" in 2 Sam 7:8–16; 1 Kgs 8:23–26) and on the misuse of power by the kings of the northern kingdom of Israel as they "continued the Sin of Jeroboam" (1 Kgs 12:26–32; 15:29–34; 16:26; 2 Kgs 3:3)

an emphasis on obedience of the law and loyalty to the covenant, including a continual struggle against idolatry, which will result in inheritance of the land and enjoyment of all of its benefits (Deut 11–12)

an emphasis on the veracity of prophetic predictions of God's judgment on and punishment of the nation for disobedience to the covenant (see Isaiah's response to Hezekiah's prayer for deliverance from the Assyrians in 2 Kgs 19:20–37)

The central theme of the Deuteronomistic Historian was the desire to demonstrate the supremacy of Yahweh over all other gods despite the historical realities of the destruction of both of the Israelite kingdoms by foreign empires. The promise is made in Deut 18:15–22 that God will raise up prophets "like Moses," who will speak in God's name and who therefore must be heeded on pain of death. This very consistent theology emphasized how obedience to the law and strict adherence to the covenant brought divine protection and prosperity for the nation. Disobedience, including idolatry and listening to false prophets, brought sure reprisal that could only be mitigated by true repentance (see 1 Kgs 21:27–29). Thus the fate of the northern kingdom was sealed when its kings continued to follow the policies of King Jeroboam. An unnamed prophet from Judah sets the tone for this condemnation by cursing the altar of the shrine that Jeroboam had set up at Bethel and predicting that human bones would be burned upon it (1 Kgs 13:1–3), a prophecy that the Deuteronomistic Historian records as fulfilled during the reforms of Judah's King Josiah (2 Kgs 23:15–16). Despite God's sending a succession of prophets from Elijah to Ezekiel to warn them of the consequences of their actions, ultimately the only thing that remained was to allow the nations to be destroyed and their people taken into exile, although a word of hope is expressed that the righteous remnant will one day return to restore the land.

16. Is Samuel a prophet?

Like Moses, Samuel is a transition figure, functioning as the last of the Judges as well as a non-Levitical priest, and as God's prophet anointing Saul as the first king of Israel. The fact that he has so many "jobs" is probably reflective of the rather disordered social character of the Settlement Period (ca. 1150–1000 BCE), and may serve as part of the argument for a king and thus greater specialization of tasks for their leaders. When Samuel initially rises to a position of authority, the Israelite tribes are threatened by the Philistines, the priestly family at Shiloh had been decimated, and the ark of the covenant had been captured. Samuel quickly points out that Yahweh's anger has been kindled by their idolatry and disobedience. He then prays for the people (intercessory role of prophet) and demonstrates that Yahweh has not abandoned the people, winning a battle and restoring the political equilibrium long enough for him to establish a judicial circuit in the central portion of the Hill Country (1 Sam 7:3–17). When the corruption of Samuel's sons (1 Sam 8:1–3) precipitates the demand for a king, Samuel dialogues with God over this change of leadership (1 Sam 8:6–9; compare Num 11:10–15). He is given the task of choosing a king, including anointing the ruler with oil (1 Sam 10:1 and 16:13). The subsequent conflicts between Saul and Samuel over the responsibilities and duties of the king in relation to the prophet (1 Sam 13–15) provide a model for many future king/prophet confrontations (see 1 Kgs 17–21). It will be difficult for the kings to humbly accept direction or order from the prophets without taking into account the political opportunities that military situations pose. For example, when Samuel relays God's command that Saul carry out a "holy war" (Hebrew: *kherem*) against the Amalekites, Saul cannot resist saving a portion of the spoil and the defeated king for a public "triumph" and sacrifice at his capital city (1 Sam 15:1–9). Samuel's anger is summed up in his exasperated statement, "Surely, to obey is better than sacrifice" (1 Sam 15:22). Each of these precedent-setting actions or roles will be a part of the careers of later prophets.

17. What is the significance of Saul's prophetic frenzy? (1 Sam 10:6–7, 10)

Despite the anarchic character of the Judges/Settlement Period, the move to establish a monarchy in Israel was not an easy or unanimous decision. Samuel's arguments against this political step include both the reality that it was a rejection of God's leadership and the protection of the divine warrior (1 Sam 8:6–8), and the fact that it would mean relinquishing local autonomy by the tribes and individual liberties by each individual (1 Sam 8:11–18). One way to smooth the path for the new leader was the creation of a tradition that established an authoritative persona worthy of the office. Of course, Saul ultimately gains the elders' respect through his military prowess (1 Sam 11), but Saul's portfolio also includes his handsome appearance (1 Sam 9:2) and his anointing by Samuel. As a further sign that Saul is open to God's spiritual counsel he spontaneously falls into the ecstatic trance state and prophecies (1 Sam 10:6–7, 10; compare the prophesying elders in Num 11:24–30). Conversely, the extended "disqualification story" that argues for the replacement of Saul's royal house by David's in the Books of Samuel makes the point that God eventually abandons Saul. The telling sign of this is that God refuses to answer him "by dreams, by Urim, or by prophets" (1 Sam 28:6).

18. Why does the prophet Nathan tell David that God does not want a temple? (2 Sam 7:1–17)

There are several political sub-plots that surface when reading this narrative. Nathan had earlier told David that God would sanction his building a temple in Jerusalem (2 Sam 7:3). In this case, David's desire to construct a temple is couched in terms of the king feeling bad that he is "living in a house of cedar" (2 Sam 7:2) while God's ark is still housed in a tent. In fact constructing a temple would mark David's growth in power and authority since monumental architecture has always been used as a form of physical propaganda. It is not surprising that Nathan would make a swift and perhaps unthinking response, catering to the wishes of his employer. A reversal then comes when God speaks to Nathan and is very adamant that a tent has always been acceptable and that David should therefore not build a temple (2 Sam 7:4–7). What emerges from this is the "everlasting covenant" that provides divine protection and authority to the Davidic dynasty and grants them the right to rule in Jerusalem forever (2 Sam 7:8–11; compare the account in 2 Chr 6:8–10). It also legitimizes Solomon as David's successor when he subsequently constructs the temple (2 Sam 7:12–13). This portion of Nathan's prophecy dates from Solomon's early reign after he wrenched the throne from his older brother Adonijah and needed a statement of divine right rule (see 1 Kgs 1:5–53). An even more pro-Solomon version of this narrative is found in 1 Chronicles 22:6–10 where David tells Solomon to build a temple and relates that God had denied him this privilege because he had "shed much blood." In fact, the costs of continuous warfare are a likely reason why David was forced to delay construction.

19. Why did Nathan use a parable to condemn David? (2 Sam 12:1–15)

Samuel warned the elders of Israel that kings have the potential to abuse their powers (1 Sam 8:11–18). David demonstrates this when he commits adultery with Bathsheba, the wife of Uriah the Hittite. When David's elaborate strategy to cover up his crime fails, he resorts to a form of indirect murder by sending a message, in Uriah's own hand, to Joab asking this Israelite general to place Uriah in the front ranks during a battle. This time the plan succeeds and after a brief period of mourning, David marries Bathsheba before her pregnancy becomes general knowledge. Such behavior is of course unacceptable under the law (adultery—Exod 20:14; innocent blood—Exod 23:7), but kings sometimes assume that they are above the law. It is therefore the task of the prophet Nathan to call the king to justice. Ironically, Nathan does

this by calling on David to serve in his capacity as the chief mag-
istrate of the people. The prophet formulates a case involving
injustice and the oppression of the weak, telling the king a juridi-
cal parable about how a rich man seizes the only thing of value
left to a poor man—a ewe lamb that was almost a family pet (2 Sam
12:1–4). The exercise raises David's anger against this injustice,
and Nathan can then, with impunity, proclaim to David, "You are
the man!" (2 Sam 12:7). The narrative then continues with the
divine imposition of sanctions against the king's house (see a sign
of this in 2 Sam 16:21–22). David pays a heavy price for his adul-
terous behavior, but the kingdom was not deprived of its
monarch. Instead, a precedent is established in which prophets are
called on by God to accuse Israelite kings of lawless acts as a
check on absolute power (see Elijah and Ahab in 1 Kgs 21:17–29).
The punishment meted out tends to be on the royal house rather
than on the individual king, but it does indicate that the biblical
writers and editors were concerned that their monarchs not be
able to act without concern for the law (compare Jezebel's attitude
in 1 Kgs 21:7).

20. Why does the prophet Gad offer David the choice of three calamities? (2 Sam 24:12–14)

The prophet and seer Gad is sent to David after the king
orders a census of his lands and people (see Gad's role as advisor
to the king in 2 Sam 22:5). David had been warned not to do this
by his much more politically savvy advisor Joab, but his hubris is
displayed by his insistence (2 Sam 24:2–9). Taking a census was
considered an act of aggression by subject peoples since it meant
that they could be more easily taxed or recruited into the army or
into labor gangs (see Archives royales de Mari 1.6:6–12 in which
tribal members flee the census takers of the king). The
Deuteronomic Historian signals to the audience that David's foolish desire is actually based on God's anger with Israel (note 1 Chr
21:1 shifts the blame for the incitement to "the satan"; see God's

anger being "kindled" in Num 32:10–13 and in the Judges cycle of stories: Judg 2:14; 3:8; 10:7). Once the census is completed, David's eyes are opened to his sin and he repents (2 Sam 24:10; compare 1 Kgs 21:27). The role of the prophet here is to deliver God's judgment on the king and to offer him the choice of three calamities (2 Sam 24:11–14). David's choice of pestilence frees the people from invasion by their enemies, but it costs the lives of seventy thousand people. God eventually relents just before Jerusalem is to be destroyed (24:15–16). David's prayer, coupled with Gad's advice to construct an altar "so that the plague may be averted from the people," expiates the king's mistake, and the favor given to David's house continues (24:18–22). David purchases the threshing floor of Araunah, the place where the angel had ended its deadly work, to build his altar (24:23–24). By purchasing the property and sacrificing to Yahweh here, David transforms it into Israelite territory (compare Abraham's purchase of the Cave of Machpelah in Gen 23:3–20). The Chronicler later ties this threshing floor to the site of Solomon's temple (2 Chr 3:1).

21. Why does the prophet Ahijah tear up Jeroboam's robe? (1 Kgs 11:29–40)

Solomon's desire to expand his power through marriage alliances lead to his committing apostasy. Despite his earlier devotion to Yahweh, he builds shrines and altars for the worship of the gods of his foreign wives (1 Kgs 11:4–8). This angers God and the prophet Ahijah is instructed to seek out a new claimant to the throne of Israel. To this point the story resembles the one in 1 Samuel 16:1–13 in which God instructs Samuel to go to Bethlehem to anoint a worthy claimant who will replace Saul on the throne. In 2 Samuel 7:8–16, however, God had promised David that his descendants would always rule over Israel and this had been confirmed in Solomon's accession to the throne (1 Kgs 6:11–13). What emerges in this narrative about Solomon's wives, however, is the historical reality of the division of the kingdom and the rise of Jeroboam as the first king of the northern kingdom of Israel. It is absolutely necessary then to demonstrate that God has had a hand in the eventual split by providing the northern tribe with a candidate for a future kingship. The older story of Samuel anointing David is therefore retold with Ahijah serving in the prophetic role. When he meets Jeroboam along the road (possibly because of the danger associated with doing it in a more public place) he uses a symbolic gesture to designate God's choice. There is some ambiguity in determining who is actually wearing the "new garment" in this passage. The Hebrew verb for "to take hold" *(wayyitpoś)*, which also appears in the story of Potiphar's wife's seizure of Joseph's robe (Gen 29:12), is generally used in passages where someone is seized or captured. Since the translation "take hold" would not fit the context when applied to oneself, it seems best to say that Jeroboam's robe is the object in question. Thus, Ahijah seizes Jeroboam's cloak from his shoulders and tears it into twelve pieces, instructing Jeroboam to take ten of them (1 Kgs 11:30–31). He will eventually be given authority over the ten northern tribes while Solomon's son Rehoboam will continue, based on the everlasting covenant with David, to rule in Jerusalem over the tribe of Judah. The twelfth piece represents the priestly tribe of Levi, which has no territory and stands apart from the political settlement. The fact that the robe is called a "new garment" may be symbolic of the new beginning for the nation.

22. Why does the unnamed prophet of Judah first curse Jeroboam and then cure his arm? (1 Kgs 13:1–10)

Initially, the scene in 1 Kings 13 appears to be a ritual performed by the unnamed prophet from Judah condemning the shrine at Bethel. The prophet's oracle against the altar disrupts the king's ceremony and actually ignores the king altogether. This is clearly a direct snub of Jeroboam's cultic role. However, the prediction of the altar's destruction in Josiah's reign can easily be separated from the rest of the narrative (vv. 2–3, 5). This section has most likely been inserted by the Deuteronomistic Historian to justify Josiah's demolition and desecration of the cultic site in the late seventh century as part of his attempt to revive Israelite nationalism. Of course, Jeroboam is upset that his dedicatory ceremony has been rudely interrupted. It is only natural that the king stretches out his arm in v. 4 to point at the prophet. This rather preemptory gesture is probably just a signal to his guards to remove a troublemaker. The subsequent withering of the king's arm (v. 4b) follows the pattern of events so common in the Elijah/Elisha cycle where a person or persons who fails to give proper respect to the Lord's representative is slain or wounded (see 2 Kgs 1:9–16; 2:23–24; 5:19b–27). Startled and frightened by his affliction, Jeroboam, much like the pharaoh in the plague sequence in Exodus 8–10, pleads with the prophet to pray to "the Lord your God" to heal his arm. This is an acknowledgment of the prophet's authority as well as recognition that God could heal him. Once Jeroboam's arm is healed he is very grateful and also obligated to reciprocate in kind. He invites the prophet to "come home with me and dine, and I will give you a gift" (v. 7). This invitation fits into the standard Middle Eastern protocol of hospitality (see Gen 18:3–5), which allows for the "guest" to refuse if there is a need to move on or some other abiding reason that transcends the granting of the favor of acceptance. Here, the prophet bases his refusal on a previous command from Yahweh that he "not eat food, or drink water, or return by the way that you came" (v. 9), and is able to snub the king once more.

23. Does the unknown prophet of Bethel actually lie to his fellow prophet from Judah? (1 Kgs 13:11–32)

The unnamed prophet from Judah cites a divine command that he not eat or return to his country by the same path when he refused Jeroboam's dinner invitation (1 Kgs 13:9). His refusal expresses the need for absolute obedience to the command of God. The irony of this position then occurs in the next episode when this same prophet disobeys God's command (13:11–32). He is invited to dinner by another prophet, a man from Bethel (13:15), and is convinced by this man's apparently updated message that allowed him to dine there (13:18). As soon as they began to eat, God speaks to the Judahite prophet, condemns him for disobedience, and states that he will not be buried in his "ancestral tomb" (13:20–22). Fulfilling this prediction, the prophet is killed on his way home by a lion and the prophet from Bethel buries him in his own tomb (13:23–32). The question is, Did the prophet from Bethel intentionally deceive the man from Judah or was this designed as a test? Clearly the Bethel prophet's assertion of an angelic message is convincing enough to break his fellow prophet's resolve, and his remorse after the death of this man is genuine, including his confirmation that the prophet from Judah had spoken a true message to Jeroboam (13:32). The purpose of the story therefore seems to be that despite the cognitive dissonance implicit in the story it is essential to recognize truth prophecy and obey God's command.

24. Why is Elijah's battle against the prophets of Baal on Mt. Carmel so critical? (1 Kgs 18:19–40)

The story of Elijah's contest with the prophets of Baal on Mt. Carmel is one of many examples of the contest motif. These stories center on the belief that the power of a nation is tied to the power of their god(s), and consist of these common elements: (1) challenge to Yahweh's divine authority, (2) response by Yahweh to meet the challenge, and (3) a clear demonstration of Yahweh's supremacy over all other gods. In every case, these narratives provide a clear example of Yahweh's power over the forces of creation and demonstrate that no god or nation has supremacy over the God of Israel.

Contest	Challenge	Response	Demonstration
Abram vs. Pharaoh (Gen 12:10–20)	Pharaoh takes Sarai, endangering covenant promise	Yahweh afflicts Egypt with plagues	Pharaoh returns Sarai, and Abram is enriched
Yahweh vs. Pharaoh	Pharaoh enslaves Israelites (Exod 1:8–14)	Plague sequence (Exod 5–12)	Red Sea crossing shows Yahweh's power over creation
Yahweh vs. Baal	Ahab and Jezebel suppress worship of Yahweh	Drought plus Elijah challenges 450 prophets of Baal (1 Kgs 18)	Yahweh consumes sacrifices and ends drought
Yahweh vs. Syria (and their god Rimmon)	Syria and its gods oppress Israel	Elisha cures Syrian Na'aman (2 Kgs 5:2–14)	Na'aman makes faith statement (2 Kgs 5:15–18)

In one of the most spectacular of these stories, Elijah champions the worship of Yahweh in the face of attempts by Ahab and Jezebel to kill the prophets. Conditions had reached such a stage that Elijah was the only prophetic voice left to speak publicly for Yahweh (1 Kgs 18:4, 7–15). Yahweh had laid the foundation for the challenge to Ahab and Jezebel by creating a three-year drought in the region (1 Kgs 17:1), an appropriate gambit since their god, Baal, was a storm god, whose devotees expected life-giving rain in season. Having inflicted this severe plague on Israel, the next step was to send Elijah to make a public demonstration of Yahweh's power in a significant spot. Mt. Carmel juts out into the Mediterranean Sea on the Bay of Acco and is the highest peak (1,791 feet) in a string of low mountains lining the coast. Of course, Mt. Carmel is also a "high place," a local cultic site that the Deuteronomistic Historian had condemned as part of Jeroboam's sin (1 Kgs 12:31). However, these Judahite editors could not contend with the popularity of the stories about Elijah and were forced to leave the locale of the story alone. A large crowd could gather to witness the events (compare the gathering in Exod 24) and this promontory could also serve as an excellent weather station from which to watch for the storm system off the Mediterranean that would bring the much-needed rain. After both sides had constructed altars and sacrificed a bull, the real contest begins as each side calls on its divine patron to accept the sacrifice and bring rain. Elijah has the amusing task of watching the 450 prophets of Baal work themselves into a frenzy to no effect. He taunts them and Baal, and then takes his turn after drenching his sacrifice with water to prevent any question of a stray spark igniting it (1 Kgs 18:26–35). The climax comes when Elijah's prayer is answered and God's fire completely consumes the sacrifice (1 Kgs 18:36–38). The unequal contest demonstrates the powerlessness of Baal and the people fall on their faces proclaiming "the Lord indeed is God" and then massacre the prophets of Baal (1 Kgs 18:39–40). As an anticlimax, the drought is ended when Ahab and Elijah eat a covenant meal on Mt. Carmel and a sevenfold sequence of watching for weather signs is concluded with the appearance of clouds and a storm marking the finale to a magnificent demonstration of divine power (1 Kgs 18:41–45).

25. What happened to Elijah on Mt. Horeb? (1 Kgs 19:9–18)

There are a number of direct parallels between the careers of Moses and Elijah including their call narratives. This adds greater authority to Elijah's prophetic role. What is particularly interesting when comparing the two scenes, however, are the differences. Although both experience a theophany on Mt. Sinai (= Mt. Horeb) and are called to perform a specific service for God, the manner in which they perceive God's presence is radically different. For Moses, his attention is attracted by a burning bush that is not being physically consumed by the flames (Exod 3:2–3). He is then addressed by God, informed that he has entered sacred space, and given the reason for God's calling him to lead his people out of captivity (Exod 3:4–10). Elijah's theophany is preceded by a miniversion of Moses's experience with the people in their trek to Mt. Sinai. During his forty days in the wilderness, Elijah receives miraculous sustenance daily (cake and water; 1 Kgs 19:5–8) in much the same way that Moses and the people received manna and quail to keep them alive (Exod 16:4–21). As Elijah sits in a cave on Mt. Horeb, God speaks to him instructing the prophet to stand on the face of the mountain to witness God "pass by" (1 Kgs 19:11; compare how Moses is allowed to see God's "goodness pass" in Exod 33:18–23). What follows is almost a contest to see whether Elijah truly knows how to discern God's presence from simple natural phenomena. Before he leaves his cave, he experiences destructive winds, an earthquake, and fire, followed by the "sound of sheer silence" (1 Kgs 19:11–12). Only when he is embraced by the silence does the prophet cover his face and step out of the cave. What he is doing here is preparing himself to be in the presence of the divine, a very dangerous proposition (see Jacob in Gen 28:16–17 and 32:30 and Gideon in Judg 6:22). By covering his face he shows humility and may therefore survive the encounter. At that point God's voice questions him and instructs the prophet on his future mission (1 Kgs 19:13–16).

26. Why does God defer Ahab's punishment? (1 Kgs 21:20–29)

The narrative describing how Ahab obtained Naboth's vineyard in 1 Kings 21 contains the best example of the motif of the King's Call to Justice (compare Nathan's use of the parable of the ewe lamb to confront David in 2 Sam 12:1–15). It appears to be an artificial reworking of the narrative by the Deuteronomistic Historian, imposing both a legal and theological stamp on the story as an indication that kings are not above the law.

Motif of the King's Call to Justice

1. King commits a crime and apparently will not be indicted by human courts

2. God or God's representative confronts the king with his crime and passes sentence

3. The king repents or is partially absolved of his guilt by other factors

4. The punishment that has been decreed is passed on to the next generation

In this case Ahab's crime is allowing his Phoenician wife, Jezebel, to engineer a false accusation against his neighbor Naboth, not speaking out against this miscarriage of justice, and then taking possession of the executed man's property (1 Kgs 21:8–16; 2 Kgs 9:26). Savoring his newly acquired land holdings, Ahab steps it off to determine its boundaries and is confronted by the prophet Elijah. What follows is a brutal indictment of the king and a devastating curse on the entire ruling family (1 Kgs 21:22–24). Frightened by such a dire prospect, Ahab makes abject repentance for his sins: "he tore his clothes and put sackcloth over his bare flesh; he fasted...and went about dejectedly" (21:27; compare the similar response by the people of Nineveh in Jonah 3:5–8). These were universally recognized mourning practices and they resulted in an interesting response from God. The Lord poses a rhetorical question to Elijah, "Have you seen how Ahab has humbled himself before me?" similar to that asked by God of the Satan in regard to Job's righteousness (Job 1:8). This signals a change of direction and the granting of temporary mercy, shifting the immediate punishment away from Ahab to "his son's days" (1 Kgs 21:19; compare a similar delay in God's wrath in 2 Chr 32:24–26). Certainly, mercy applied even in such a heinous case as this would have brought hope to other sinners (see Ps 51) and would have put other kings on notice that they must abide by the law just like everyone else.

27. Can one prophet contradict another prophet? (Micaiah in 1 Kgs 22:5–28)

Embedded in this narrative are two complementary lessons about how to discern true prophets. The basic rules on determining true from false prophets are found in Deuteronomy 18:18–22. A true prophet must speak in the name of Yahweh, never in the name of another god, and must speak only those words that Yahweh has spoken to him or her. Presuming to speak in God's name without having received a direct message from the deity is punishable by death. The ultimate proof that a prophet is speaking God's words is to be found in whether "the thing does not take place or prove true" (18:22). The difficulty in 1 Kings 22 is that Ahab's royal partner, Jehoshaphat, the king of Judah, does not trust the veracity of this message from prophets who are members of Ahab's court (22:5–8). This forces Ahab to summon an unaffiliated prophet, Micaiah ben Imlah, "who never prophesies anything favorable" to the king (22:8). The kings then create a very intimidating spectacle for Micaiah's benefit, placing themselves on their thrones at the city gate with Ahab's four hundred court prophets prophesying before them (22:10). Ahab's chief court prophet, Zedekiah, is very adamant about their positive message and punctuates his performance with a pair of iron horns to graphically indicate how God will "gore the Arameans" and give Ahab's military a victory (22:11). In the face of such pressure, it is not surprising that Micaiah initially agrees with Ahab's court prophets (22:15), despite his disclaimer that he would only speak "whatever the Lord speaks to me" (22:14; compare Balaam in Num 22:38). Once the king cajoles him to speak truly, however, Micaiah recounts a vision in which God is sitting upon his throne surrounded by the divine assembly. In this vision God asks "who will entice Ahab, so that he may go up and fall at Ramoth-gilead?"

(22:20), and a volunteer is chosen to speak a false message to the court prophets. Zedekiah is outraged at this slander and slaps Micaiah, accusing him of actually being possessed by a "lying spirit" rather than the court prophets (22:24). Micaiah responds that the truth of his message will be determined by whether the king is able to "return in peace" from the battle (22:28). This qualifies the episode as an example of what psychologists call cognitive dissonance, a dilemma of discernment created by two contradictory statements that each appear to be true (compare 1 Kgs 13:11–32). Just as Deuteronomy 18:22 states, the only way to determine the truth of the matter and whether the court prophets have been suborned by God's intention to destroy Ahab is to await the outcome of the battle. While Micaiah waits in prison (22:27), Ahab and Jehoshaphat march off to war, and, in the end, Ahab's mortal wounding and death prove who, in this situation, is the true prophet (22:29–37).

28. Why does a prophet work miracles for his own followers? (2 Kgs 4; 6:1–7)

Two things in particular link Moses and Elijah/Elisha: (1) the extreme danger to the viability of the covenant community in their time, and (2) the use of miracles to show the power of Yahweh. Thus, the plagues that are inflicted on Egypt function as a miraculous contest among Yahweh, the pharaoh, and the gods of Egypt demonstrating to the Israelites who really is God and the benefits that they can expect from faithfully worshiping this deity. Further examples of this include the Red Sea crossing (Exod 14) and God's miraculous provision of water, manna, and quail during the wilderness trek (Exod 15:22–16:21). In the period of the divided monarchy, Ahab and his Phoenician wife, Jezebel, endanger the worship of Yahweh by "killing off the prophets of the Lord" (1 Kgs 18:4) and emphasizing the worship of Baal and Asherah (1 Kgs 16:31–33). Elijah/Elisha must rely on a group of supporters referred to as the "company of the prophets." They may simply be the faithful remnant within the land, who continue to worship Yahweh (see 1 Kgs 19:18). It is also possible that they are disciples or companions of the prophet, who carry out missions when he requires assistance. For instance, in 2 Kings 9:1–3 Elisha instructs one of the company to go to Ramoth-gilead to anoint Jehu as king over Israel. Such a task ordinarily would be carried out by Elisha (see 1 Kgs 19:16), but he is too well known and since this mission will precipitate a civil war it may need more discretion (see Jeremiah's use of Baruch in Jer 36:4–8). As a result of their loyalty and service the company of the prophets deserved some compensation and thanks. This is supplied on several occasions by Elisha not only as a form of gratitude (as he does in rewarding the childless Shunammite couple for their hospitality in 2 Kgs 4:8–37), but also as a demonstration of the rewards that can be obtained by those faithful to Yahweh. Thus Elisha provides a widow of the company with a miraculous jar of oil to sustain her in her poverty (2 Kgs 4:1–7), and on two occasions he provides a meal for the company (2 Kgs 4:38–44): in one case purifying a poisoned stew and in the other miraculously multiplying a small amount of food so that it feeds one hundred men (compare Jesus's feeding of the five thousand in Matt 14:13–21). In yet another example of the care expressed by the prophet for these men, Elisha caused an iron ax head to float saving one of them from falling into debt because the valuable ax had been borrowed (2 Kgs 6:1–7).

29. Why should a foreigner who worships other gods consult a prophet of Yahweh? (1 Kgs 5)

This narrative contains two familiar themes: the motif of Contest between Gods and the theme of universalism. The focus is on a non-Israelite, Na'aman the Syrian general who has been inflicted with leprosy. As is generally the case with high-level individuals who have exercised a great deal of authority and do not wish to have their careers curtailed early, Na'aman is not con-

tent to accept his affliction without a fight (compare the leprous
beggars in 2 Kgs 6:3–10). Presumably he sought a cure in his own
country, but like any polytheist he is also open to the idea that a
god of another land may be able to help him (see how Israel's
injured king, Ahaziah, sent messengers to inquire of the Philistine
god Baal-zebub of Ekron in 2 Kgs 1:2). Thus he takes the advice
of an Israelite slave girl in his household to seek out the prophet
Elisha and goes through the difficult diplomatic process needed to
secure safe passage between combating nations (2 Kgs 5:2–7).
The contest between gods is initiated when Elisha tells the king of
Israel to send Na'aman to him so "that he may learn that there is
a prophet in Israel" (2 Kgs 5:8). The Syrian general is accompanied by chariots and an entourage of guards, all signs of his
authority, but instead of gaining an audience with the prophet he
is forced to communicate with a servant. It must have been difficult to restrain his temper at this breach of social protocol, and he
was further incensed by the command to bathe himself in the
Jordan River in order to be cured (2 Kgs 5:9–10). He not only
wanted the prophet to appear in person; he also wanted a show of
power, like a magician who will "wave his hand over the spot"
(5:11). Of course, the intention here is to humble the proud general by asking him to take the cure on faith, to do something he
may believe is foolish, but to do it on the indirect command of
God's prophet. Desperate to find relief, he cools his anger and
once again accepts the advice of his own servants to follow the
prophets instructions and is cleansed of his disease (5:13–14).
Overjoyed at this change in his condition, Na'aman makes a statement of faith acknowledging "that there is no God in all the earth
except in Israel" (5:15). His announcement functions as the mark
of the theme of universalism, which employs non-Israelites as the
witnesses to God's supreme power (see Rahab in Josh 2:8–11).
Even so Na'aman falls back into his role of "great man" and
wants to pay a huge price for his cure. This is countered by
Elisha's refusal since the cure had come from obedience and had
thus been earned by Na'aman. Thus Na'aman is humbled again

and begs for a gift himself, asking for "two mule-loads of earth" so he can take back to his country a symbolic portion of God's land that can be incorporated into an altar to Yahweh. He also asks dispensation for his actions as aide-de-camp to the king of Syria when that person goes to worship the god Rimmon, assuring the prophet that this is an expected task but no longer represents his devotion to that god (5:16–18). The conclusion drawn from the story is that Yahweh has defeated Rimmon and the gods of Syria by curing Na'aman and thus certified the belief that there is only one God "in all the earth."

Three

Late Monarchy Period

30. Why do written prophets suddenly appear in the mid-eighth century?

Up until the end of the Elisha cycle of stories in 2 Kings 13:21, the chief political rivals to Israel and Judah have been small neighboring kingdoms, with Syria (Aram) the most powerful of these nations. What changes at the beginning of the eighth century BCE is the reemergence of an international superpower, the Assyrians. Over the next century, the Assyrian rulers continually expanded both direct control as well as economic and political hegemony over all of Mesopotamia and Syria-Palestine. Their royal annals and monumental inscriptions and the biblical account include escalating encounters that indicate how the smaller nations were intimidated, forced to pay tribute, and increasingly came under the sway of the Assyrians (see 2 Kgs 15:19–20, 29; 16:7–10; 17:3–6). The only power holding them in check was Egypt, instigating intrigues and revolts within the small states on the fringes of Assyria's empire in Syria-Palestine (see the Rabshakeh's speech in 2 Kgs 18:19–1). In the end, the Assyrians conquered Israel in 721 BCE, deporting a large proportion of its population, and they devastated Judah, destroying its towns and cities and exacting heavy payments from King Hezekiah to spare Jerusalem in 701 BCE (2 Kgs 18:14–16). In the face of this mounting threat to the very existence of the nations of Israel and Judah, the level of prophetic activity markedly increases. However, the miracle-working prophets of the ninth century are replaced by individuals whose emphasis is on speaking out in public places and providing logical arguments for obedience to the covenant with Yahweh. Perhaps because their message is more elaborately presented and because oral tradition is beginning to give way to written records in Israelite culture, the words of the prophets are collected, organized, and preserved as

45

testimony to the truth of God's power. Of course, much of what they have to say is unwelcome since it emphasizes the failure of the people to uphold their obligations under the covenant. They harangue the people in an effort to explain that God has not failed or been defeated when the nations of Israel and Judah are oppressed or conquered by foreign nations who worship other gods. This message is a form of theodicy, a rationalization for why God allows things to happen that do not benefit the chosen people. Writing down the words of the prophets and creating a body of prophetic literature that can be preserved and referred to by later generations provides a broader picture of salvation history for the people, demonstrates God's control over historical events, and serves as a continual warning of the consequences of violating the covenant.

Amos

31. What are the principal themes in the Book of Amos?

Amos is called as a prophet during the first half of the eighth century BCE, during a period of time in Israel's history of relative peace and prosperity. The encroaching Assyrian empire had expanded as far as Damascus and then stopped temporarily to consolidate its gains before pushing further to the south and west. The result was that Israel's chief rival among the smaller states, Syria (Aram), was removed and Israel was able to concentrate for a few decades on building up its commercial activities and gaining greater influence over its smaller neighbors. The rush of business opportunities, coupled with the creation of large farms as poor farmers were driven into debt and off their land, and the lack of an immediate military threat combined to make the wealthy and influential in Israel too complacent. Amos, as an outsider from Tekoa in Judah, does not rejoice with the rich over their good fortune, nor does he take comfort in the lavish rituals and sacrifices at the royal shrine in Bethel. Instead, this prophet from the rural populace uses very simple language, much of it pastoral in character (see the vision of "summer fruit" in Amos 8:1–3), to condemn the rich and powerful for abusing their privileges and failing to care for the poor and powerless in their society. He employs two primary themes: (1) social criticism and (2) hollow worship. As noted in the responses below, Amos is very specific in his charges of social abuse and makes it clear that the offenders will see their world of self-indulgence turn into ruins (Amos 4:1–3; 5:10–11). He cannot fathom their inability to see that taking advantage of the poor (forcing them into debt slavery and ignoring their basic needs; Amos 2:6–8) is a violation of the covenant. Furthermore, he condemns their attitude that carefully orchestrated ritual is a substitute for true devotion and humble worship of God (Amos 5:21–24; compare Mic 6:6–8). He warns them that their time of peace is about to end and the only way they can save themselves is to "seek good and not evil" (Amos 5:14). The prediction of Israel's destruction at the hands of the Assyrians does leave open a small hope that God will use a sieve in judging the people, allowing the evil ones to drop through and be destroyed while a remnant will remain to eventually restore the kingdom under the leadership of a Davidic ruler (Amos 9:9–11).

32. Why does Amos appear so negative and unsympathetic with his audience? (Amos 1:1; 4:1–3; 5:10–13)

To explore the negative attitude in the Book of Amos it is first necessary to point out this prophet's background. He is a small farmer from Tekoa, a village of perhaps 100–150 people, situated about seven miles south of Jerusalem on the edge of the Judean wilderness. For such a small community to survive in this marginal location, the inhabitants would have had to carefully manage their resources, develop an appreciation for the talents of everyone in the community, and find ways to overcome disputes that could lead to conflict or lost production. Like most rural farmers, Amos diversified his activities, herding sheep (1:1) and cultivating fig trees on his small holding (7:14). He undoubtedly worked hard and he knew hardships brought on by drought, disease, and financial difficulties that could lead a family into debt slavery. When his call to serve as a prophet comes, Amos is forced to leave all that was familiar and travel north into Israel to the king's cult center at Bethel. Separated from his land and his neighbors, the prophet is faced with an entirely foreign social situation and what results is a very critical and angry response to what he sees as social and religious abuses. It is not surprising then that his oft-repeated phrase in referring to the covenant-breakers in Israel equates them with those "who trample the head of the poor into the dust of the earth" (Amos 2:7; 5:11; 8:4). He seems to be particularly angry with those who are so self-indulgent that they utterly fail to empathize with those who are hungry, cold, or cheated by the courts. In his metaphorical labeling of the rich wives of the elite of Samaria as "cows of Bashan," the prophet sums up his indictment of persons who can "crush the needy" while calling on their husbands to meet their every desire (Amos 4:1). Amos has no sympathy for those who lack any vestige of basic human kindness and he predicts an ignominious death for them with their tortured bodies thrown unceremoniously on a dung heap (Amos 4:2–3). As a farmer himself who may have also had to deal with the greed of the wealthy in his own land, Amos warns those who have built fine houses with the taxes and debt payments extorted from the poor that they will not live in them nor enjoy the fine vintages that they have worked to create (Amos 5:11–12; compare Zeph 1:13).

33. Why does Amos repeatedly refer to those "who trample the head of the poor into the dust of the earth"? (Amos 2:7–8; 5:11–12; 8:4–6)

Several of the prophets have catchphrases or signature statements that they repeat to emphasize their message and perhaps to differentiate themselves from other prophetic voices. Amos chooses to distinguish his message by boldly stating that there can be no justice in a land in which the powerful choose to "trample the head of the poor into the dust of the earth." He is able to cite numerous instances, using language very similar to that found in the twentieth-century BCE Egyptian *Tale of the Eloquent Peasant,* chronicling how judges take bribes and "turn aside the needy in the gate" (Amos 5:12; compare Isa 29:21) or "put more [grain] in their own ration" (Matthews and Benjamin, *Old Testament Parallels,* 234). Amos points to those who are willing to take "levies of grain" from the poor in order to enrich themselves (5:11). He condemns those who choose to deceive consumers with "false balances" or who freely sell "the sweeping of the wheat" instead of providing an honest measure (8:5–6). The petty swindles of merchants in the marketplace are a symptom of a sick society that lacks basic civility or concern for either the law or one's fellows. This is demonstrated in Amos's charges in 2:7–8. Here, he describes how the powerful push the poor aside as they walk unconcernedly through town to the shrines of false gods where they lay with cult prostitutes and then sleep through the night before the altar of these foreign deities on "garments taken in pledge." It is interesting that the prophet completes his litany of crimes with one that provides a clue to the cupidity of Israel at that time. The law is very clear that when a day laborer puts up his cloak as collateral, a pledge that he will provide an honest day's work in the fields, that cloak must be returned to him at night so that he may sleep in it (Exod 22:26–27). The fact that this is not an unusual practice is attested by the *Yavneh Yam Letter,* which contains the plea of a day laborer that his cloak is returned along with his dignity (Matthews and Benjamin, *Old Testament Parallels,* 355–56).

34. Why are the New Moon and the Sabbath so important for Amos's judgment on Israel? (Amos 8:4–6)

Unlike their neighbors, Israelite merchants were constrained from doing business during either the weekly Sabbath celebration

(Exod 20:8; 23:12) or during the New Moon festival that marked the beginning of each month (Num 10:10; 29:11). This latter festival figures into a number of biblical narratives, including David's escape from Saul's palace (1 Sam 20:24–25) and the Shunammite's journey to seek Elisha's help for her stricken son (2 Kgs 4:23). The two festival days are often mentioned together (Isa 1:13; Hos 2:11) perhaps indicating that they are the most frequent interruptions in daily commerce and thus would be a thorn in the side of greedy businessmen who find it more desirable to add to their own fortunes than to honor and thank God for the harvest that has made them rich. In this case, they grumble over the lost opportunity to arrange commodity transactions in the grain market and to make their fraudulent sales to unwary customers (Amos 8:4–6).

35. How does Amos compare to the prophet Samuel in his preaching?

Since Amos is from Judah, he had a dim view of Israel's rival shrines at Dan and Bethel, its non-Levitical priesthood, and its "false rituals" based on Jeroboam's sin (see 1 Kgs 12:26–33). In addition, as a representative of the rural population, he, like the prophet Micah at the end of the eighth century, is more attuned to the Mosaic covenantal tradition that emphasizes obedience over ritual practice. In his condemnation of worship in Israel, Amos is quite sarcastic, inviting the people to "come to Bethel—and transgress" and to "bring your sacrifices every morning, your tithes every three days" (5:4). In other words they can go through the motions all they want, but it will do no good. This is because their festivals and "solemn assemblies" have become displeasing to God, a cacophony of sound without meaning because there is no justice in the land (5:21–24). Both Amos's sarcastic attitude and his call for strict obedience to God's word rather than orchestrated ceremonies that only feed the ego of the officiants sound similar to Samuel's harsh assessment of Saul's failures in 1 Samuel 15 to carry out the holy war against the Amalekites. He has set aside some of their choice animals and the king of the Amalekites to serve as a public sacrifice (1 Sam 15:7–9). This self-aggrandizing behavior was the catalyst for Samuel's biting sarcasm that he is inexplicably hearing the bleating of sheep when there should be none there (1 Sam 15:14). Saul and his family are condemned and Samuel sums up his judgment of the king's actions by making the plaintive statement, "Surely, to obey is better than sacrifice" (1 Sam 15:22). By comparison, Amos points to silenced prophets (2:12), ignored warnings (4:6–9), "houses of ivory" built by the wealthy at the expense of the poor (3:15; 6:4), and illegal high places and sanctuaries (7:9), and he sees a total lack of interest in obedience to God's command. Thus, like the extinction of Saul's House, Israel will be abandoned and taken into exile along with its false gods (5:26–27).

36. Why does the priest Amaziah react so violently to Amos's message at Bethel? (Amos 7:10–13)

It must have been difficult for the authorities in Bethel, men who had been appointed by the king to serve as priests, to listen quietly to Amos's harangue against them and the ritual practices that they conducted in the "king's sanctuary." They had a vested interest in maintaining their position as the appointed guardians of religious activities, and therefore one of their chief priests, Amaziah, comes forward to ridicule Amos's prophetic status and to tell Amos to leave them in peace (Amos 7:12). He first reports Amos's words to the king, charging the prophet with trying to instigate a conspiracy that will be dangerous to the crown (7:10), and then publicly confronts Amos. He suggests that Amos is simply a troublemaker who hopes to "earn his bread" by acting the role of a seer, duping the people into believing that he carries a message from God. Contemptuously, the priest dismisses the man for "operating without a prophet's license" and orders him to return to his own land. Amos's simple reply takes the bluster out of Amaziah's words, retorting that he, unlike the priest, has no need for a prophetic genealogy since he was called by God from his work as "a dresser of sycamore trees" to speak to the people of Israel (7:14–15). Interestingly, the process of slicing open the fig releases ethylene gas causing the fruit to increase in size and ripen. Amos's angry words can be compared to the knife at work, cutting into Israel for their lack of empathy for the poor and their acts of social injustice at all levels. However, the nation's pain can in turn spark a more mature understanding and acceptance of their covenant responsibilities. Amos completes his response to the priest's challenge with a prediction of doom for Amaziah and his family in the coming conflagration that will consume the nation (7:17; compare Jeremiah's response to Pashur in Jer 20:2–6). This sort of confrontation demonstrates the difference between those who make their living by directing sacrifices and conducting the business of the temple and prophets who do not draw a salary and who are directed by God to point out abuse, corruption, and mismanagement.

Hosea

37. What are the principal themes in the Book of Hosea?

The message of the Book of Hosea is intermeshed with the approaching crisis at the end of the eighth century BCE that will mark the final days of the nation of Israel. The prophet, who is an Israelite and therefore much more sympathetic to their inevitable doom than Amos, pleads with his people to return to strict compliance with the covenant, to renounce all other gods, and to recognize their obligation to "know God" by trusting in his law and his command. The most remarkable of his themes is presented in the form of a marriage metaphor in which he is instructed to marry a woman who will become unfaithful to him, a representation of God's covenant with the nation that has been violated by the people's worship of other gods (chapters 1–3). The marriage produces three children who are given symbolic names, each more devastating than the last and functioning as a demonstration of God's growing frustration and ultimate rejection of the nation. An additional theme that stands out in the book is his harsh indictment of kings and priests in Israel. This is in fact a critique of the sin of Jeroboam, which has led the people away from God. He points to the "calf of Samaria" (8:6; 13:2) and Israel's leaders, who "build palaces" (8:14) and encourage the people to worship at "multiple altars" (8:11). He condemns these practices that reflect the leadership's desire for political and personal power and have precipitated the coming crisis (5:1–2; 7:1–10; 8:4–6). He also reminds them that since they lack true knowledge of God they will not manifest the quality of "steadfast love" (6:6) that flows from an understanding of the benefits of the covenant. They have forgotten the salvation history of the nation and God's role as the one who "fed them in the wilderness" and defended them against their enemies (13:4–6). For this reason God will turn away from the people and allow these rebels to "fall by the sword" (13:16). They are indeed lost, just as a child that refuses instruction and will not obey its parents requires punishment (11:1–7). Despite this justifiable divine anger, however, a strand of forgiveness and longing for a return to proper covenantal compact with the people also runs through Hosea's warnings. Just as Hosea's wife, Gomer, can be returned to her husband if she renounces "her lovers" (2:14–23), the people, if they hear the call to repentance and "return to the Lord," can be revived and once again know the Lord (6:1–3).

38. Why does Hosea use a metaphor for marriage to make his points? (Hos 1–3)

While it is impossible to gauge whether Hosea's marriage metaphor had an immediate effect on his audience, it is apparent that it is the only extended oracle that remains intact in the Book of Hosea. Much of this collection of prophetic sayings was compiled after the destruction of Israel by the Assyrians in 721 BCE. For this metaphor to survive suggests that it was considered among the most important of Hosea's sermons and that it does speak to the lasting impact of his plea for the nation to return to their role as the faithful "wife" of God. Its basic simplicity is another argument for its likely effect on his audience. The very transparency of a human marriage and its troubles over infidelity as a metaphor for the covenantal relationship between God and Israel and its history of idolatry needs little explanation. There is some question about whether Gomer is a prostitute at the time of her marriage to Hosea (1:2) or whether she gradually becomes unfaithful (2:2) after producing three children for her husband. To be sure, if one considers the full range of Israelite history, they came from a polytheistic background before God offers Abram the opportunity to accept the covenant with Yahweh (Gen 12:1–3; 17:2–8). Once they established themselves in the land of Canaan, however, they failed to adhere to the command to "have no other gods before" Yahweh (Exod 20:3). Like Gomer, they have taken other "lovers" (= other gods) and now must be punished for their foolish trust in powers that cannot provide the "grain, the wine, and the oil" that a husband pledges to his bride (Hos 2:8). Israel's drunken revelry and joy in the abandoned behavior common in festival celebrations to the god Baal have clouded their judgment and they must face up to a wrathful God/husband, who in his anger will strip them of the land's fertility, a primary quality of the covenant agreement (2:11–13; see Hosea's return to this theme of Israel's riotous prostitution to other gods in 9:1–2). The domestic crisis, that involves the husband pleading with his children to intercede with their mother (2:1–2), as well as threats to cast her naked into the street for all to see her guilt and his shame (2:3), are not so outlandish that an Israelite audience could not sympathize with the couple's troubles. Plus the desire for reconciliation and the offer to take back a cherished wife if she will pledge her fidelity to husband, totally renouncing her former indiscretions, may be more than many men would do, but does stand out as a clear example to the people of divine mercy (2:14–23).

39. What is the significance of the names given to Hosea's three children? (Hos 1:4–9)

The marriage between Hosea and Gomer produces three children. Each is given a symbolic name that represents a facet of God's growing anger with the unfaithfulness (both religious and political) of the people of Israel. The naming of the firstborn son, Jezreel, speaks to the ruling dynasty in Israel and, as in Hosea 7:11–13, warns the monarchy against reliance on any power other than God's. Israel's eighth-century kings are descended from Jehu, a general who had been anointed by Elisha's messenger and given divine sanction to overthrow the House of Ahab (2 Kgs 9:1–10). The "blood of Jezreel" (Hos 1:4) refers to Jehu's demand that Ahab's seventy sons be executed and their heads be brought to him at Jezreel as a sign by the nobility of Israel that they now accepted Jehu as their king (2 Kgs 10:1–11). By naming his son Jezreel, the prophet is putting the ruling house on notice that it was God who had given them the right to rule the nation and that same God could take away their sovereignty as well, a prophecy fulfilled by the Assyrian destruction of Samaria in 721 BCE (2 Kgs 15:29). When Hosea's daughter is born, she is given the name *Lo-ruhamah,* which means "not pitied" (Hos 1:6). This is the unswerving judgment of God on a nation that no longer deserves pity or forgiveness. Hosea is particularly concerned with the lack of proper leadership shown by the kings and priests of the nation. He likens the activities of princes to "those who remove the land-mark," a gross violation of property rights of every member of the covenant community (Deut 19:14). Priests have fed on the sin of the people and the result is "swearing, lying, and murder, and stealing and adultery" (Hos 4:2, 8). When Hosea's third child is born, this second son is given the most devastating name possible for an Israelite. He is named *Lo-ammi,* "not my people" (1:9), and this suggests that the prophet believes this is not his child, but rather a "child of whoredom" (2:4). Israel prided itself in being the chosen people (Deut 7:6–11), but now their legitimacy is called into question and their claim to protection and prosperity under the covenant is revoked.

40. Why does Hosea equate the "knowledge of God" with "steadfast love"? (Hos 6:6)

In this passage, Hosea employs two strands of tradition: wisdom and the legal framework of covenant obligation. In biblical wisdom literature the words "to know" (Hebrew: *yāda'*) or "knowledge" (Hebrew: *da'at*) are very often paralleled in the text with "understanding" (Hebrew: *t'bûnâ*). Thus a knowledgeable man has understanding (Prov 17:27), and one who lacks "human understanding" will also not have "learned wisdom, nor have knowledge of the Holy One" (Prov 30:2–3). Hosea therefore calls on the people of Israel to express the desire to "press on to know the Lord" (6:3), to learn that when they sow righteousness, the reward is God's "steadfast love" (10:12). The second half of Hosea's parallel statement turns on the legal obligations attached to covenant service. Hosea uses the term for "love" (Hebrew: *hesed*) that is most often associated with God's love for the people (see Exod 20:6, 34:6; Num 14:19; Deut 7:12). He had noted earlier that the people's love is as ephemeral as the morning mist that burns away as soon as the sun touches it (Hos 6:4). Now, paralleling Samuel's statement to Saul in 1 Sam 15:22, the prophet completes his equation by explaining that what God desires is their love, not their sacrifices (compare Amos's condemnation of "hollow worship" in 5:21–24). This understanding would be theirs if they possessed the knowledge of God. Unfortunately, because the priesthood and the Israelite monarchy "have forgotten the law," the "people are destroyed for lack of knowledge" (4:6; compare Isa 1:3). They are therefore "hewn by the prophets" and must face God's judgment because they do not know God's desire (Hos 4:5).

41. What strong images does Hosea use to reinforce his judgment oracles?

Hosea employs a series of comparative statements to demonstrate how God has cared for the people of Israel and has received poor treatment from them in return. For instance, the nation's original value or appearance that attracted God's attention is likened to "grapes in the wilderness," to the "first fruit on the fig tree," to a "young palm," and to a "luxuriant vine"—all pleasant to the traveler or farmer who sees them for the first time (9:10, 13; 10:1). In each case, however, their apparent beauty is marred by the people's idolatry, a practice that is certain to draw God's wrath upon them (9:11–12, 15; 10:2). Like the marriage metaphor in chapters 1–3, the parenting image in Hosea 11 provides a simple comparative image and an insight into Israel's relationship with God that any parent can understand. The perceived ingratitude of children to their parents is a common experience (11:1–3). Inexplicably, a child who has been loved, cared for, and trained can take a path directly opposite to the one the parent desires. Since this is a farming society, dutiful childcare is likened here to the treatment of valued farm animals, whose work is valued and protected by law (Exod 23:4–5; Deut 25:4). Just as a child is taught to walk and is protected from harm, these creatures are "lead by cords of human kindness" and their yoke is eased (Hos 11:4). Ultimately, the theodicy of judgment that appears in these repeated images of Israel's refusal to listen to God's words and their outright rejection of the call to repent their idolatry can only lead them to being driven from their house and left like a dried up plant whose roots have withered (9:15–17).

FOUR

ISAIAH

42. Why do some people refer to three different Isaiahs?

The Book of Isaiah is a long and complex collection of narrative, poetry, and prophetic pronouncements. Its familiar vocabulary and themes run throughout the book, but there are indications that different time periods are represented in the final chapters and that has lead scholars to surmise that the work should be divided at least into two and possibly three sections. First Isaiah (chapters 1–39) represents the period from approximately 740–681 BCE during the final days of the northern kingdom of Israel and the crisis of Assyrian invasion for Judah. He describes specific historical events during that period and points out the role of Assyria as the "rod" of God's anger (10:5). Second Isaiah (chapters 40–55) open with a celebration of the end of the Babylonian exile in 540 BCE, voicing words of comfort and assuring the exilic community that its "penalty is paid" and they should now begin a glorious procession back to Zion (40:2–3). This portion of Isaiah provides, in four Servant Songs, a theodicy explaining the cause, purposes, and value of the exile to those who are now encouraged to return and rebuild Jerusalem. A final section, referred to by some scholars as Third Isaiah (chapters 56–66), speaks from the perspective of the returned exiles, who have by 515 BCE rebuilt the temple in Jerusalem, reestablished the priestly community, and are struggling to meet the challenges of restoring the land to productivity. Dissatisfied with the exclusionist direction the priesthood is taking the community, this voice of Isaiah reminds them once again of the dangers of ritualized worship and fasting without real meaning, and the real value attached to sharing their food and shelter with the poor while honoring the Sabbath (58:6–14). Since only about twenty-five years separates Second and Third Isaiah, it is possible that both sections of the text were produced by the same author or group of authors.

What is clear is that the wide gulf of time from 686 to 540 is too broad for First Isaiah to have survived. Instead, his ideas, his themes, and his love of Jerusalem survive and are carried on by disciples or students of his prophetic oracles (see 8:16). Speaking in his name they continue the Isaiah tradition into new social situations for the people and provide guidance and reassurance that God remains a force in their lives while they are in exile and after the return to the Persian province of Yehud.

43. What are the principal themes in First Isaiah? (chapters 1–39)

Isaiah of the eighth century BCE is a contemporary of several other prophets, including Hosea, Micah, and Zephaniah. Unlike them, however, Isaiah has a high social status that allows him easy access to kings (7:3–9; 38:1–8) and the temple (6:1–5). Like Nathan in David's court, Isaiah stands as an authoritative voice, one that can be consulted and relied upon in times of crisis (37:2–7). His focus is on Judah, Jerusalem, and the House of David. In the midst of the fear and chaos created by the approaching Assyrian threat during the last quarter of the century, Isaiah repeatedly predicts a time when a righteous king of the line of David will emerge and rule in justice over the people (9:6–7; 11:1–5; 32:1–8). Despite current difficulties caused by weak rulers like Ahaz, who refused to listen to Isaiah's reassurances and instead turned to Assyria for help against his enemies (7:10–17), the nation's hope still lies in the hands of a ruler who trusts in God's words (28:16) and obeys them (see the description of Hezekiah in 2 Kgs 18:3–7 and the righteous king's prayer in Isa 37:14–20). Since the fall of the northern kingdom occurs during Isaiah's prophetic ministry, a theodicy is called for to explain this disaster and the subsequent exile of many of the inhabitants of both Israel and Judah to distant portions of the Assyrian empire. He chides Israel for its arrogance and failure to seek the Lord, condemning those "who teach lies" and lead the people astray, and now sends judgment on them in the form of the despoiling Assyrians (9:8–10:4). But Isaiah never leaves the people without hope of return and restoration. A strong theme of retribution on the nations that have been used to punish Israel (10:5) runs throughout the book and is contained in a series of "oracles against the nations" (chapters 14–24). These oracles include a litany of charges and predictions of doom that will come on "the day of the Lord" when the nations will be confronted by the reality of true power and God will put an end to their pride, their arrogance, and their useless altars (see 13:9–11; 17:7–9). Then the exiles will return, guided by the "root of Jesse" (a reference to the Davidic king; 11:10), with Judah reversing her fortunes to the extent of "taking captive" their captors and ruling over other nations (14:1–2; see the victory song in Isa 26). Even the scattered peoples of Israel will "on that day" return to "worship the Lord on the holy mountain at Jerusalem" (27:12–13). In this way, according to the prophet, the "wounds" of division that had doomed the northern kingdom and contributed to its idolatry and misrule will be healed (30:23–26), and the nation's people will all be joined in correct worship and devotion to God's temple on Zion and ruled by the true heir of David (32:1–8; 33:17–22).

44. What are the basic elements of Isaiah's call narrative? (Isa 6)

Isaiah's call narrative follows the pattern set in Moses's call before the burning bush (Exod 3:1–4:17). Like Moses, he experiences a supernatural manifestation of God's presence (a theophany), in this case within the temple precincts (sacred space—compare Exod 3:4) and marked by earthquake and smoke (Isa 6:1–4). This powerful appearance of the divine is daunting to both Moses and Isaiah and both makes excuses in order to avoid God's call to service. Since Isaiah is a priest, his demure or excuse centers on ritual purity and the inability of any mortal lips to speak the sacred words of God (6:5). God's purpose is not to be denied, however, and neither Moses nor Isaiah is allowed to decline. Each is given an empowering response, and Isaiah's lips are purified by a seraph, who, in this vision, cauterizes them with a hot coal taken from the altar (6:6–7; compare Exod 4:15–16). All either man can then do is to accept their call and leave themselves open to God's command (6:8). The unusual aspect of Isaiah's call narrative, however, and the way in which it differs from that of Moses is found in the charge given to the prophet. His message is one that is not to be comprehended. In fact it is to dull their minds, stop up their ears, and shut their eyes (6:9–10). This sounds completely counterproductive, but it fits the time of crisis in which it is given. Because the people have always proven themselves to be "stiff-necked" (Exod 32:9; 34:9) and have not responded to previous prophetic warnings, they are now to be consigned to their fate. Isaiah's instructions suggest that his message inevitably will fall on deaf ears and unperceiving eyes in a time when fools reign and the wicked refuse to "turn and be healed" (6:10). Isaiah is shocked and asks God "How long?" these conditions will persist; the answer provides him with little comfort since God assures him that the destruction will continue until only a tiny remnant remains (6:11–13). Contained in this remnant, however, is the "holy seed" of restoration and that must content the prophet until God's judgment has been fulfilled. In fact, a later oracle in Isaiah 32:3–5 provides a reversal of the conditions at the time of his call narrative. On that future day when a righteous king reigns (32:1), the land will be restored and the "eyes of those who have sight will not be closed, and the ears of those who have hearing will listen."

45. What makes the Song of the Vineyard in Isaiah 5 such a powerful oracle?

The large number of instances in which the Hebrew prophets mention the vineyard or use it as a metaphor for the Israelites points to the high value that viticulture had in their daily lives (see Jer 2:21; Ezek 17:5–6; Hos 10:1). Its economic importance made it a natural metaphor for stability and prosperity (2 Kgs 4:25; Isa 36:16). And the loss of the vineyard's production easily served to demonstrate the height of religious and economic disorder (Jer 8:13; Joel 1:11–12). In his Song of the Vineyard, Isaiah sketches out in painstaking detail the very familiar aspects of working a hillside vineyard. The first step in the process is the construction of terraces. To make best use of the rains, a series of terraces would have been built, creating strips of land that followed the contour of the hill or encircled it. Because the slopes of the Judean hills were badly eroded the farmers had to construct retaining walls and transport new topsoil from elsewhere to fill the terraces. Thus when Isaiah describes the vineyard as lying on "a very fertile hill" (5:1), it is because the local farmers have done the backbreaking labor needed to make it so. Once the farming surface has been prepared, the vineyard must be planted with cuttings. The term *(soreq)* that Isaiah uses here for "choice vines" signifies a variety of red grapes associated with the Soreq Valley (Judg 16:4). Continual care during the growing season must be given to prevent the growth of moisture-sapping weeds, briars, and thorns (Isa 7:25). During the winter months of the first six years of growth (Lev 25:3) the maturing vines are pruned with a short, curved knife (Isa 2:4) to remove a portion of the previous season's growth (4 Macc 1:29) and to insure proper nourishment of the remaining grape clusters (2 Esdr 16:43). The industrious vineyard owner, who realizes the dangers of small animals (Song 2:15) and travelers to his crop, takes extra measures to protect the vines and their fruit (Prov 24:30–31). For this purpose, Isaiah mentions the construction of both a hedge and a stone wall, indicating the expensive and determined efforts by the owner to guard the vineyard from harm. For the same reason, a watchtower is constructed to shelter the laborers and to serve as the post of a sentinel to give warning of marauding bands of animals or humans. The final step in the process of creating a complete installation is the carving out of a wine vat in the soft limestone of the hillside that would be used in the threading process during the harvest. It is during the harvest that the grapes are tasted to determine their readiness to be taken to the winepress. This would be the stage at which the owner or his overseer could make a judgment (5:2c; Gen 40:11). If the grapes have a sour taste, they may have been picked too early in the growth cycle (perhaps in July or August) when they have not yet produced as much sugar. But the question asked here is, "What more was there to do for my vineyard that I have not done in it?" (Isa 5:4a). Metaphorically the vine is at fault. Just like the wicked that are characterized by Job as a malicious plant (15:33), this vine is acting unnaturally. Such evil cannot be borne, for the land is precious and the time expended by the owner and the laborers is unrecoverable. Thus the Song of the Vineyard concludes with a very harsh sentence for this "crime" that decries the land's value and suggests abandonment and revocation of all interest or concern in future dealings. The fabric of the vineyard—its terraces, walls, soil, and vines—are to be thrown down and left in a state that can only be compared to the condition of a city that has been abandoned by its God/gods. With the terraces destroyed, the soil will erode away and what remains will only nurture thorns and weeds. In a world that must make the best use of its land, the terraces will eventually be rebuilt and the vineyards will be replanted. This scene of restoration, common in Isaiah (compare Isa 32:12–20), will make it possible for the new vines to escape the fate of the first vineyard.

46. What is the historical background of Isaiah's Immanuel prophecy? (Isa 7)

At the time that Isaiah predicts the birth of the child Immanuel, Judah is faced with the double threat of invasion by the forces of King Pekah of Israel and King Rezin of Syria (Aram). This Syro-Ephraimite War (730s BCE) was based on the desire of the smaller states on the western border region of the Assyrian empire to break away from their imperial master. The Assyrian ruler,

Tiglath-pileser III (744–727), had imposed heavy tribute payments on them and abolished the autonomy of the local states, incorporating them into the empire and they responded by trying to reassert their national identities in periodic revolts. To be effective, however, all of the small states needed to stand together or the Assyrian army would pick them off easily one by one. Israel and Syria formed a coalition, but King Ahaz of Judah refused to join them, fearing Assyrian reprisal. In an effort to force Judah to conform to their political plan and to remove Ahaz from his throne, the two kings invaded Judah. They were initially repulsed (Isa 7:1), but Ahaz knows that they will try again. It is at this point, as the king and his entourage make an inspection of the defenses and the water supply of the city of Jerusalem that he is confronted by Isaiah and is presented with a message that seems impossible to accept. The prophet offers, on God's behalf, a sign that the king need not be concerned with these enemy nations for they will be dealt with by the divine warrior. Of course, no king or politician can stand idly by while the nation is in danger. Ahaz has already made his decision before Isaiah speaks to him, sending to Assyria for help. However, the prophet persists even in the face of Ahaz's refusal. He points to one of the women accompanying the king and predicts a very short-term resolution of the matter. Using the standard annunciation formula (predicting a birth and naming the child; see Gen 16:7–12), the prophet states that within the brief period from the child's birth until he knows the difference between right and wrong both Israel and Syria will be defeated and Judah will be impoverished (7:14–17). This can be no more than thirteen years, the age of adulthood for Israelite males, and the Assyrian Annals record the destruction of Israel's capital at Samaria in 721 BCE and the ravaging of Judah's towns and villages. As for the name of the child, Immanuel, "God is with us," it is not designed to reassure the people but rather to warn them that God is the instigator of their punishment. He is not intended to be a messianic figure like the child in Isaiah 9:6–7, and the Hebrew text makes no claim that his mother is a virgin (compare the messianic reinterpretation of this passage in Matt 1:23). More important than this particular child in the context of the war is the demonstration of God's power over events. In a series of "on that day" pronouncements (7:18–25), God is identified as the sole power behind Assyria's military victories, and this massive empire is reduced to being simply a "razor for hire" (7:20).

47. Why does Isaiah refer to Assyria as "the rod of God's anger"? (Isa 10:5)

It is essential to Isaiah's theodicy that the armies of Assyria and their gods not to be seen as the victors over Israel and Yahweh. Whatever temporary accomplishments the Assyrian kings may achieve and despite their arrogant boasting, a common feature of their royal annals, they have not acted on their own. They have simply served the purpose of "the rod of God's anger" (10:5), as a "razor for hire" (7:20), as "mighty flood waters" (8:7) filling the land of Judah with suffering as the marauders take their spoils. Of course, other nations, including the Arameans and the Philistines (9:12), were also drawn into the general feasting on Israel's and Judah's weakened defenses. However, once God's wrath is complete the instruments of destruction will then be dealt with so that the "ax [may not] vaunt itself over the one who wields it" (10:15).

48. What is meant by Isaiah's prediction of a "shoot from the stump of Jesse"? (Isa 11:1–9)

Jesse is David's father (1 Sam 16:1–13), but in Isaiah's vision of the "stump of Jesse," the metaphor refers to both the apparently dead nation, cut off at the ground by the ravaging of the Assyrian army, and to the monarchy that has failed to provide leadership in the time of crisis. What every farmer knows, however, is that stumps do not die immediately after the tree is cut down. For several years their roots continue to draw life from the soil and green shoots of growth project from the stump as new branches. Therefore what appears to be dead will spring forth with a new vigor to assist in the restoration of the nation under the leadership of a righteous king (compare the "dry bones" image in Ezek 37:1–14). David is differentiated from other rulers by the infusion of God's spirit that will guide him in wisdom, under-standing, and knowledge (11:2), and he will in all things look to the Lord for direction. These qualities stand in direct contrast to the stubbornly obstinate attitude displayed by Ahaz and other kings of Judah, and they set an idealized standard for leadership that few kings will ever be able to approach. Very likely Isaiah's vision of the just king, who judges from an inner quality of righ-teousness rather than by appearances alone, is aimed at convinc-ing Ahaz's son Hezekiah to take up the Davidic ideal of leadership so that the Eden-like state of affairs described in 11:6–9 can come into being. The Deuteronomistic Historian's account of Hezekiah's reforms (2 Kgs 18:1–8) and the manner in which the king shows a willingness to take counsel with Isaiah (2 Kgs 19:1–7) add to this expectation of greatness. He is even described as one who "was right in the sight of the Lord just as his ancestor David had done" (2 Kgs 18:3). The reality of the sit-uation, however, is that Hezekiah's reforms are short-lived and he is succeeded on the throne by a child, Manasseh, who is easily manipulated by the pro-Assyrian forces in his court. Isaiah's hope is left unfulfilled, although it is revived for a time a century later when King Josiah takes up the reform agenda originated by his great-grandfather (see the evaluation in 2 Kgs 22:2).

49. Why does Isaiah walk around naked for three years? (Isa 20)

In the final quarter of the eighth century BCE, the rivalry between Assyria and Egypt revived over control of the commer-cial activity and raw materials (cedar logs and incense) of the Levantine coast. As a result, the Egyptian dynasts attempted to establish links with the Arab tribes of the Sinai and with the Philistine and Israelite kings. One result of their political maneuvering was the revolt in 713 BCE of Azuri, king of the Philistine city-state of Ashdod against the Assyrians. The Assyrian emperor Sargon II responded quickly to this challenge and conquered the city in the next year. He put his own puppet ruler on the throne and transferred Ashdod's status into an Assyrian province under the direct control of the empire. At the time of the Ashdod Revolt, Hezekiah undoubtedly was approached by representatives of the beleaguered city and by the Egyptians and asked to join a coalition fomenting a general rebellion against the Assyrians. This situation, much like that in the 730s that had eventually resulted in the destruction of Israel, required a warning from Isaiah of the consequences Hezekiah could expect if he joined in the fight. The prophet, who is already wearing sackcloth as a sign of mourning for the nation, engages in a radical enacted prophecy, stripping himself naked and walking about barefoot (Isa 20:2). He does this to punctuate his message that foreign entanglements will only lead to being taken captive into exile. In literally baring his shame and vulnerability, Isaiah portrays himself as a slave or a prisoner of war, who has been stripped of personal identity and freedom. Since the Assyrian Annals do not include any mention of action taken against Judah at this time, it may be assumed that Hezekiah took Isaiah's advice and laid low while the Assyrian war machine conducted its business along the coast of Philistia.

50. What is Isaiah's "Little Apocalypse"? (Isa 24–27)

Embedded within First Isaiah is a brief section (chapters 24–27) that probably dates to the sixth century and falls within the context of the fall of Jerusalem to the Babylonians in 587 BCE. Its placement here by the biblical editors may be based on connections between the oracles against the nations in Isaiah 13–14 and the prediction of a general destruction of nations in Isaiah 28–34. It has been termed the "Little Apocalypse" because it contains some elements of apocalyptic literature (see question 94, pages 139–40), including cosmic battle (24:21–23), a celebratory feast on the holy mountain (25:6–10), and the raising of the righteous dead (26:14, 19), but it is not consistent with later apocalyptic texts (see Zech 9–14). The themes included in these chapters begin with a divine judgment. There is a reversal of creation (compare Isa 33:7–9), which will "lay waste the earth," cause great human suffering, and break down the defenses of the "city of chaos" (24:1–13). Once God has demonstrated his power over the "host of heaven" (24:21), there are two hymns of praise for turning the evil city "into a heap" that will never be rebuilt (25:1–5), and for creating a "strong city" that will now house the "righteous nation" (26:1–6). The cycle of destruction and restoration is then completed with an eschatological vision of God's triumph over Leviathan (27:1; Ps 74:12–14), a return to the vineyard metaphor of Isaiah 5:1–7 (Isa 27:2–11), and concluding with a return of the exiles to worship in Jerusalem (27:12–13).

51. Why are Hezekiah's advisors so frightened by the Rabshakeh's claims? (Isa 36:4–10)

Hezekiah would not be able to escape the attention of the Assyrians forever. He experienced the aftermath of the destruction of Samaria in 721 BCE and stood aside during the Ashdod Revolt of 713–712 BCE. However, the biblical account records that Hezekiah instigated a series of religious reforms that included the elimination of local high places, the destruction and removal of sacred poles dedicated to Asherah and other gods, and even the dismantling of the bronze serpent that had been cherished as a relic since the time of Moses (2 Kgs 18:4; compare the longer list of reforms in 2 Chr 31). The centralization of worship in Jerusalem and the elimination of the worship of some foreign gods would probably not occasion a direct response by the Assyrians. However, Hezekiah does rebel against the king of Assyria when he attempts to expand his borders by invading

Philistine territory as far south as Gaza (2 Kgs 18:7–8). Of course, the exact timing of Hezekiah's reform and political break with Assyria is not noted in the biblical text, but it most likely occurred during the interregnum period after the death of Sargon II in 705 BCE and the ascension of Sennacherib to the Assyrian throne. Many of the Assyrian provinces revolted during this time and Egypt once again attempted to gain allies and to support rebellion as a means of further weakening its rival. Once Sennacherib had put down the most dangerous of these revolts in Babylon, he turned to the consolidation of his power throughout the empire. This included a campaign in 701 BCE in Judah, which the emperor records at length in his Annals. Sennacherib describes how he "laid siege to 46 of [Hezekiah's] fortified cities...and to the countless villages...using earthen ramps and battering rams." Details of the campaign include the capture of the western border city of Lachish and the taking of over 200,000 prisoners and the imprisonment of "Hezekiah in Jerusalem like a bird in a cage" (Matthews and Benjamin, *Old Testament Parallels,* 192). It is after the utter destruction of Lachish that Sennacherib sends his personal ambassador, the Rabshakeh, to Jerusalem to command Hezekiah to surrender the capital and once again accept Assyrian rule (2 Kgs 18:17–37; Isa 36). The arguments employed by the Rabshakeh demonstrate that theodicy is not unique to the biblical prophets. This military commander stands outside the city walls at the same point where Isaiah had confronted Ahaz (Isa 7:3; 36:2) and taunted Hezekiah's officials. He chides them for putting faith in an alliance with Egypt, that "broken reed" that will puncture the hand of any who pick it up (36:6), and he even offers to "loan" them two thousand horses if they can put riders on them (36:8). Most devastating, however, are his claims that their predicament has been caused by Hezekiah's reforms that had deprived God of his high places and altars throughout the country (36:7). The people of Jerusalem can therefore not expect an angered God to protect them or relieve the siege (36:16–18). In fact, the Rabshakeh claims, I would not even be here except that

"The Lord said to me, 'Go up against this land and destroy it.'" In this way both the gods of the Assyrians, who have conquered all other nations and their gods (36:19–20), and the God of Judah have combined their powers to threaten Jerusalem's survival. Hezekiah's officials realize how believable the Rabshakeh's arguments are to the ears of Jerusalem's people. They still believe in the religious maxim that gods and nations fight in war and that their God could indeed summon a foreign power to correct the lawless or foolish actions of their king. The desperate officials plead with him to speak in the diplomatic tongue, Aramaic, so that the common people will not be frightened and possibly revolt against their king (36:11), but the Assyrian is not about to give up his advantage and his speech becomes even more filled with despairing scenarios. Ultimately, both the biblical and the Assyrian accounts agree that the siege is ended when Hezekiah pays a huge ransom for the city (2 Kgs 18:14–16; Matthews and Benjamin, *Old Testament Parallels*, 192).

FIVE

MICAH

52. What are the principal themes in the book of Micah?

Micah is an exact contemporary of Isaiah. He experiences the same historical events that lead to the fall of the northern kingdom of Israel to Assyria in 721 BCE and the invasion of Judah by Sennacherib's army in 701 BCE. However, his perspective of these horrendous happenings is from that of the countryside. He is a rural farmer from the small town of Moresheth, just over four miles northeast of Lachish and in the vicinity of the Philistine city of Gath. Thus he would have had an all-too-close-up view of the burning, looting, and general mayhem associated with military campaigns. This may help to explain why his prophetic message differs from that of Isaiah and why he focuses primarily on social criticism and on a condemnation of the cities and their rulers that have brought destruction down on the heads of the common people of the countryside. The Book of Micah, like many prophetic books, does not follow a logical sequence and each successive poetic oracle is not necessarily predicated on the one before it. Perhaps the easiest way to characterize the themes in Micah is to divide them into (1) social criticism from a rural perspective (1:2–2:11; 3:1–12; 6:9–16; 7:17), (2) a covenant lawsuit against the nation (6:1–8), and (3) a future restoration, with a focus on a royal messiah figure (4:1–5) and on God as a caring shepherd (2:12–13; 7:8–20). The prophet, who discounts the words of false prophets by saying that they are a disgrace, proclaims his own credentials as one who has been filled "with the spirit of the Lord" (3:7–8). His emotions run the gamut from extreme grief over war's upheavals (1:8–9), to a hot anger with the political centers (3:9–12) and a dishonest and grasping society (6:11–12), to a sublime vision of a coming time of peace when all suffering will come to an end and God's mercy will "cast all our sins into the depths of the sea" (7:19).

53. Why does Micah condemn the cities of Jerusalem and Samaria? (Mic 1:2–16)

Perhaps because he represents the rural perspective of the small towns and villages of Judah, Micah expresses a simple view of politics, assuming that all that is evil in society is a product of the large urban centers of Samaria and Jerusalem. In his theodicy explaining the destruction of Israel's capital and the deportation of its population, he sees God, not the Assyrians, treading "upon the high places of the earth" and transforming Samaria into "a heap in the open country" as a just recompense for a prostitute's idolatry (1:5–7). The steady progression of destruction through the Shephelah to the Judean Hill Country (from Gath to Lachish) leads directly to the gate of Jerusalem and to Zion (1:10–13). The social evils of the wealthy, who covet fields and houses and cheat the covenant community out of its rightful inheritance (2:1–3), are indicative of a society that has lost its way and must now face the homelessness of exile (2:10). The rulers of both nations, who should uphold the law, instead "abhor justice and pervert all equity" (3:9–10). Because even the priests and prophets will only teach or speak for a price, "Zion shall be plowed as a field; Jerusalem shall become a heap of ruins" (3:11–12). Micah's very shocking predictions of the destruction of Samaria and of Zion/Jerusalem must have had a chilling effect on the people since his words are quoted a century later during the trial of Jeremiah (Jer 26:18).

54. What is the basis for Micah's covenant lawsuit in Micah 6:1–8?

Covenant lawsuits take various forms in the prophetic literature. Nathan employs a parable to indict David for his adultery with Bathsheba (2 Sam 12:1–15), and Isaiah uses the Song of the Vineyard to call on the people of Judah and Jerusalem to judge whether anything more could have been done to care for or to warn the nation (Isa 5:1–7). In Micah's version of this genre he calls on the mountains (i.e., all creation) to stand as witnesses to the particulars of the Lord's "controversy with his people" (6:1–2). As a preface, the salvation history of the nation is briefly recited including the exodus from Egypt, the prophecies of Balaam in Moab (Num 23:4–12), the zealous action of Phineas to cleanse the people of idolatry at Shittim (Num 25:1–13), and the miraculous crossing of the Jordan River at Gilgal as the people began their conquest of Canaan (Josh 4:19–24). The prophet then employs a sarcastic tone, suggesting, like Amos (4:4–5), that the people try astronomically magnifying their offerings (Mic 6:6–7). This is merely a taunt that sets up the familiar conclusion that what the Lord's covenant truly requires of the people is "to do justice, and to love kindness, and to walk humbly with your God" (6:8). Like Samuel (1 Sam 15:22), Amos (5:21–24), and Hosea (6:6), Micah reiterates the prophetic admonition that it is better to obey God's word than to sacrifice. Although not directly connected to the lawsuit, the remainder of chapter 6 does provide a bill of particulars against Israel for following the unwise counsel of Omri and Ahab and for tolerating dishonest business practices that oppress the poor (6:9–16a). For these crimes they will be forced into exile to work for the benefit of others, and the memory of their fate will become "an object of hissing" for future generations (6:16b).

55. Why does Micah speak of a messianic king and a divine shepherd in his vision of a future restoration to the nation? (Mic 4:8; 5:2–5; 7:14–15)

It is a cardinal feature of prophetic literature that once God has purified the nation for its iniquities a remnant will return under God's direction to restore the land. Micah uses this theme in 4:6–7, with God pledging to gather the scattered peoples and the lame, transforming them into a strong nation. He reprises the promise of the return of the exiles in 7:11–17, portraying God as the divine shepherd, who will feed the flock "as in days of old"

(7:14; compare Ezek 34:11–31). What is interesting is that Micah provides yet another image of restoration—one that includes the future of the nation under the leadership of a messianic king (5:2–5). What seems strange about this is that this prophet has little good to say about Jerusalem or the succession of Davidic rulers that have reigned over the nation. However, his prophetic oracles do contain a reference to a messianic king coming out of Bethlehem, who will restore the nation and provide the leadership needed to prevent a repetition of their current troubles (see the quotation of this passage in Matt 2:6 as the birthplace of the Messiah). The tie to Bethlehem, David's hometown (1 Sam 17:12), links this oracle to the Davidic monarchy, but it also takes the audience back before David was king to the time when he was first identified by Samuel as God's chosen. It also links true leadership to the social values of the small village culture, once more shunning the effects of urban bureaucratic government. Furthermore, the promise that he will be guided by God's majesty to "feed his flock" and bring them peace and security (5:4–5) is an excellent parallel to the messianic king described in Isaiah 9:6–7, who will also establish "endless peace."

Six

Minor Prophets of the Seventh Century

56. Why are there no specific prophetic voices recorded during the reign of Manasseh?

When Hezekiah's son Manasseh came to the throne of Judah at the age of twelve in ca. 687 BCE (2 Kgs 21:1), his government initially would have been placed in the hands of a regency council made up of advisors. These men had witnessed the invasion of Judah during Hezekiah's reign and they realized that the Assyrian campaign had been the direct result of the king's reform movement. It is quite likely that they would have witnessed the Rabshakeh's speech (Isa 36), which chronicled Hezekiah's crimes against his Assyrian master; this put into sharp focus the realities of the international political situation, which required the Assyrians to maintain a secure buffer zone (Syria-Palestine) between themselves and Egypt. Thus Manasseh would have been counseled to accept Judah's place within the Assyrian empire, to quietly pay tribute and provide any other lip service demanded of a vassal ruler. This would help explain the long list of charges made against Manasseh by the Deuteronomistic Historian (2 Kgs 21:2–16). Embedded in this list is evidence of a resurgence of the worship of the gods of Canaan, with altars constructed in Jerusalem to "all the host of heaven" (21:3–4). While there is no direct evidence that Manasseh imported Assyrian gods and rituals, it is quite probable that some acculturation took place for political purposes and this would have been acceptable in the polytheistic climate of the times. No specific prophetic voice is raised against Manasseh during his long reign, although there is a brief mention of God assuring the prophets that the evil he has done will bring such a harsh divine reprisal that it will make "the ears of everyone who hears of it tingle" (2 Kgs 21:12). The charge made against Manasseh that he "shed very much innocent blood" may be a reference to his suppressing the prophets of Yahweh (compare Ahab's policy in 1 Kgs 18:4). If so, the individuals may have had to wait until this king and his Assyrian masters had passed from the scene.

57. What are the principal themes in the Book of Nahum?

When empires die their vassals rejoice over their temporary freedom until a new empire is born. The Book of Nahum contains the voice of a prophet from Judah, who prophesies the destruction of the Assyrian capital of Nineveh and with it the bonds of vassalage that have enmeshed Judah for over a century. Nineveh in fact fell to a coalition of Median and Babylonian forces in 612 BCE and therefore Nahum dates to the decades immediately prior to this time. The task of the prophet is to make it clear that Assyria's demise is based on a judgment by Yahweh, "a jealous and avenging God" (Nah 1:2). Nahum builds his argument by first providing a description of how God's power is manifested in a theophany (divine appearance) of whirlwind and storm that "dries up the rivers" and makes the "mountains quake before him" (Nah 1:3–5). By using these images of power, Nahum also supersedes any possibility of others ascribing the coming events to Baal, the Canaanite storm god. In what sounds like a propagandistic tone designed to strike fear into the hearts of its citizens, Nahum then provides a graphic depiction of the destruction of Nineveh by an irresistible army whose chariots will careen through the streets while no one can stop the savage plundering of the city (Nah 2:3–12). The prophet then continues his vision of devastation with two judgmental statements prefaced by the phrase "I am against you, says the Lord of hosts" (2:13; 3:5). In each he points to the "countless debaucheries of the prostitute" that has enslaved other nations (3:4) and who now will have its naked shame exposed for the entire world to see (3:5–6). To conclude his theme of retribution, Nineveh is reminded that it is no better than the cities it has destroyed in its own triumphal period. Like them, the Assyrians will face exile no matter how much attention they give to preparing for the coming siege (3:12–17).

In the end, all of Nineveh's victims will "clap their hands" over its utter destruction (3:19).

58. What are the principal themes in the Book of Zephaniah?

Zephaniah voices his prophecies during the early reign of King Josiah of Judah (640–609 BCE). Like Nahum, he rejoices over the fall of Assyria (2:12–15), and looks forward to a purge of the leadership of Judah that has led the people astray (see the Deuteronomistic Historian's assessment of Manasseh's rule in 2 Kgs 21:9). Like Amos, Isaiah, and Jeremiah, his contemporary, Zephaniah's message includes a condemnation of the surrounding oppressor nations (chapter 2). His use of this theme includes the admonition to the people of Judah to "seek righteousness, seek humility" (2:3) in order to prevent themselves from being caught up in the sweeping away of the chaff. For Moab, Ammon, and the Philistine cities are to be left without inhabitants, the coastal plains left to serve as pasturelands and Transjordan will be plundered by the remnant of Judah. However, he also predicts the approaching divine judgment of Judah and Jerusalem as well (1:4; 3:1–7). He makes particular use of the "Day of the Lord" theme, a day of judgment, a day to fear the wrath of God, and a day of "distress and anguish" (1:7–18). The "Day of the Lord" is also employed in Zephaniah's apocalyptic vision of restoration. On that day the remnant of nation will have been purified, the proud will have been removed from their midst (3:11), and the people shall "lie down and no one shall make them afraid" (3:12–13). The prophet concludes his message with hymns of joy, for "on that day" Zion and Jerusalem will be exalted and their fortunes restored (compare similar language in Pss 47 and 97).

59. What are the principal themes in the Book of Habakkuk?

The Book of Habakkuk provides no biographical data about the prophet and it is only possible to date his message by his reference to the rise of the Neo-Babylonians (Chaldeans) that began as early as 625 BCE and reached full prominence in the years between 612–600 BCE. Structurally, the book consists of two distinct units: (1) the Pronouncement (Hebrew: *maśśa'*) of the Prophet, which includes a dialogue between Habakkuk and God (Hab 1:1–2:4) and a set of woe oracles (2:5–20), and (2) a Psalm of Lament (Hebrew: *šigyōnôt*) in chapter 3 that asks God for deliverance and contains the theme, also found in chapter 2, that God will eventually bring all forms of oppression to an end. Particularly interesting in section one are the complaints made by the prophet (1:2–4, 12–17) asking God "how long" the violence must continue and questioning why the wicked are allowed to prosper at the expense of the righteous (see similar charges of social injustice in Amos 2:6–12; 4:1; 8:4–6). These complaints are interspersed with God's responses (1:5–11; 2:1–20), which include the statement that the Chaldeans have been "roused" (1:6) to remove the Assyrian oppressors. The people of Judah are then reassured that God also intends to bring judgment on the pride-filled Chaldeans for their extortions and greed. Using of the Hebrew particle *hôy* as the preface to each of his series of woe oracles, Habakkuk indicts those who "heap up" (2:6) unjustified wealth by cheating the righteous and pillaging the weak (compare Isaiah's use of judgmental woe oracles in Isa 3:9; 5:8; 45:9). Chapter 3 can be identified as a psalm by the inclusion of standard hymnic forms: a superscription, the rubric *Selah* dividing segments of the prayer, and an orchestration comment or colophon that directs the choir master to use stringed instruments (3:19b). The psalm itself contains a variety of themes, including creation (3:3–4; compare Ps 104:1), cosmic struggle (3:8–11; compare Isa 34:2–3), and a victory hymn celebrating Yahweh's supreme control of nature's forces (3:8–15; compare Ps 114).

60. What are the principal themes in the Book of Obadiah?

The twenty-one verses that compose the Book of Obadiah provide a brief summary of a number of familiar prophetic themes. These include the promise of divine judgment on Israel's oppressors (vv. 8–9), the "Day of Yahweh" theme (vv. 8, 15), the forced drinking of the "cup of wrath" metaphor (v. 16; Jer 25:15; Ezek 23:33), celebration of Zion as the seat of God's people and divine majesty (vv. 17, 21), and the ultimate kingship of Yahweh over all of the world (v. 21). Taken as a whole, Obadiah contains an excellent example of the prophetic oracle against a nation, in this case Edom (compare Jer 49:7–22). Since there are no direct historical references in Obadiah, it is possible that the targeting of Edom is intended as a representation of all enemy nations rather than just a single neighbor (see v. 15). However, the mention of the old conflict between the ancestral brothers Jacob and Esau (vv. 10, 17–18; see Gen 27:41; 33:1–17) as well as the pronouncement of doom on those who "stood aside" while Jerusalem was plundered (v. 11) and "gloated over your brother" (v. 12) do suggest a more specific wrong done to Judah dating to the period of 587–586 BCE when Jerusalem was captured and destroyed by the Neo-Babylonians (compare Ps 137:7–9; Lam 4:21–22). In the midst of this disaster, Edom may well have taken advantage of the opportunity to claim a portion of Judah's territory.

61. Why does Josiah consult the prophet Huldah? (2 Kgs 22:13–20)

At the critical moment when King Josiah wished to obtain divine certification that the Book of the Law that had been uncovered during the renovation of the Jerusalem Temple was in fact authentic (2 Kgs 22:10–11), it appears somewhat unusual that the chief priest, Hilkiah, and the other advisors of the king chose to consult an otherwise obscure female prophet named Huldah (2 Kgs 22:13–14; 2 Chr 34:22). At the time (622 BCE), more prominent individuals including Jeremiah, Zephaniah, and Habakkuk could have been consulted. The key may be that Huldah, the only female prophet mentioned in the Book of Kings, is the wife of a member of the king's royal bureaucracy, Shallum, "keeper of the wardrobe" (2 Kgs 22:14). This would mean that Huldah was a court prophet and therefore someone who would be more likely to provide a positive response to the king's query (see Nathan in 2 Sam 7:3 and Ahab's four hundred court prophets in 1 Kgs 22:6). Still, she does not appear in her speech to these high-ranking questioners to be intimidated and speaks as authoritatively as other prophets do in the name of "the Lord, the God of Israel" (22:16). Characteristic of the theological agenda of the Deuteronomistic Historian, her oracle begins with an indictment of the people of Judah based on their failure to obey the words of the Book of the Law and provoking God with their idolatry (2 Kgs 22:16–17). She has a more charitable assessment of Josiah's kingship, taking note of his acts of contrition and humble prayer of forgiveness. She promises him a peaceful death before God's judgment falls on the nation (2 Kgs 22:18–20). In fact, Josiah dies at the Battle of Megiddo in 609 BCE in an abortive attempt to delay the advancing Egyptian army of Pharaoh Necho II (2 Kgs 23:29–30). The Judean king had hoped to prevent any assistance being given to the Assyrians in their final fight against the Medes and Neo-Babylonians at Carchemish.

SEVEN

JEREMIAH

62. What are the principal themes in the Book of Jeremiah?

Jeremiah's career as a prophet spans the period from 626 to 586 BCE. During this time, this man from the small village of Anathoth, three miles from Jerusalem (see its association with the exiled Levitical priests under Abiathar in 1 Kgs 2:26), witnessed the heady events associated with Josiah's reform and the king's early attempts to restore the old Davidic kingdom (2 Kgs 23:1–27), the political debacle following Josiah's death at Megiddo in 609, and political domination of Judah by Egypt and Babylon (2 Kgs 23:33–24:7). His prophetic message resounded during the reigns of Josiah's sons providing a theological backdrop to the events leading up to Jehoiakim's revolt against Nebuchadnezzar in 600 that resulted in the capture of Jerusalem in 598 BCE and the initial exile of a portion of the nation's nobility and royal house as hostages. Jeremiah continued to prophecy during the reign of Zedekiah and the second siege of Jerusalem that marked the end of the monarchy, the destruction of the city and the temple, and the exile of a large segment of Judah's population to Mesopotamia in 587 BCE (2 Kgs 24:8–25:21). Such a long period of active prophetic service produced a large body of oracles, sermons, and biographical material. Unfortunately for modern readers, this is not organized in chronological order and his activities and themes must be sorted out by regrouping the chapters (see chart below). As might be expected during such a tumultuous period, Jeremiah's principal themes include God's judgment on the nation, a theodicy explaining the Babylonian capture and destruction of Jerusalem (Jer 27; 37–38), and a long series of oracles against foreign nations representing God's eventual revenge on these oppressors (compare Isa 13–23; Ezek 25–32). Once it becomes clear that the exile from Judah is a long-term reality, Jeremiah, in his letter to the exiles (29:1–23), provides a new theological path for the people who have been stripped of the temple and the sacrificial system. He also sets a tone for the eventual return from exile in his redemption of a field from a kinsman during the siege of Jerusalem (32:1–15) and in a series of oracles in what is referred to as the Book of Consolation (Jer 30–33). Naturally, anyone as controversial as Jeremiah raises the ire of the authorities and he faces both official condemnation by the priestly officials (20:1–6; 26:7–11) and imprisonment by the king (37:11–21). He also has to face a challenge from other prophets, like Hananiah, who predict a swift end to the exile and continued opposition to Babylon (Jer 28). It is a testimony to his perseverance and the compulsion placed on him by God to speak (20:7–9) that Jeremiah was able to survive for such a long period as a social pariah and as a witness to the end of his nation's hope to be spared God's wrath one more time (see 26:18–19).

Time Divisions	Segments of Jeremiah	Themes and Content
From Josiah to Jehoiachin (626–598 BCE)	Jer 1–26, 36	call narrative, Temple Sermon, enacted prophecies, Baruch's mission to the Temple
Zedekiah (598–587 BCE)	Jer 27–29, 32–35, 37–39	letter to exiles, contest with Hananiah, redeemed field, theodicy of surrender to Babylon
Period post-586 BCE	Jer 40–45	Gedaliah's governorship, Jeremiah taken to Egypt
Unspecified date	Jer 30–33, 46–51	Book of Consolation, oracles against the nations

63. How does Jeremiah's call narrative compare to that of other prophets? (Jer 1)

Jeremiah's call narrative has some distinct similarities to that of both Moses and Isaiah. Like them, he experiences a theophany identifying him as God's chosen, even while in the womb (1:5), to speak to the nation. Jeremiah's initial response is, like other prophets, to make excuses for why God must have made a mistake. He points to his extreme youth, his lack of training as a speaker, and the likelihood that no one would listen, but this is quickly pushed aside with the explanation that God will give him the words and the protection needed to make his message effective (1:6–8; compare Exod 4:10–12). Then in another remarkable similarity, Jeremiah's mouth is empowered when touched by God's hand (1:9), a parallel to the purifying of Isaiah's lips with a hot coal by a seraph in Isaiah 6:7, Ezekiel's consuming a scroll of prophecy (Ezek 3:1–3), and the appointment of Aaron as Moses's "mouth" to speak to the people (Exod 4:15–16). Where a difference does occur with previous call narratives, however, is in Jeremiah's message since it deals with a set of events unlike anything previously faced by the nation. Jeremiah is appointed "over nations and over kingdoms, to pluck up and to pull down, to destroy and to overthrow, to build and to plant" (1:10). These are the powers ordinarily exercised by kings (see how Marduk, the chief god of Babylon, is invested with all power in the *Enuma Elish* creation story [Matthews and Benjamin, *Old Testament Parallels,* 15]). In the face of the inevitable demise of Judah's monarchy, a new voice of authority is necessary for the remnant of the people to survive the coming cataclysm. Jeremiah is charged with standing like an impregnable "bronze wall" so that his steadfast message can be delivered unfailingly in the face of opposition and ridicule. The people must come to believe that the enemy (Babylon) is coming and that Jerusalem will be besieged by "all the tribes of kingdoms of the north" (1:14–19).

64. Why does Jeremiah give his most important oracle in the Temple itself? (Jer 7 and 26)

Jeremiah's "Temple Sermon," (contained in chapters 7 and 26) is portrayed as the first major public appearance by the prophet. It occurs in 605 or 604 BCE, over twenty years after Jeremiah is called as a prophet, and during the critical days of King Jehoiakim's reign when Babylon is about to regain control over Judah. The prophet is ordered to stand in the gate of the Jerusalem Temple on a festival day when he can expect a large crowd will be making its way into the temple precincts. This is an excellent setting for a public address and it contains an important symbolic backdrop for Jeremiah's words, which are actually an attack on the sacred character of the temple and its priestly community. As the crowd moves forward to make their sacrifices and present their petitions to God, Jeremiah startles them with the statement that their standard, threefold litany on entering the temple gate, "The Temple of the Lord," is in fact only "deceptive words" (7:4). They have no meaning because the people have driven God from his temple with their manifold violations of the stipulations of the covenant. God must literally plead with them to "amend your ways and your doings, and let me dwell with you in this place" (7:3, 5–7). The prophet then lists the commands found in the Decalogue and asks them whether they truly believe that they can violate all of these divine laws and then "come and stand before me in this house…and say 'We are safe!'" (7:10). Should any doubt his words, he suggests that they go to Shiloh where God's ark had once rested and his presence had been manifest (1 Sam 1:3; 4:4), and see that it, like the northern kingdom, now lies in ruins because of "the wickedness of my people Israel" (7:12, 14–15). Jeremiah's challenge to the temple authorities results in his nearly being lynched by an angry mob (26:7–9). He is subsequently brought to trial before the king's advisors and is acquitted based on their recognition of his office as a prophet of Yahweh and the precedent of previous prophets who had predicted the city's downfall only to have God show mercy when the people acted with righteous repentance (26:10–19; note the quotation from Mic 3:12 in Jer 26:18).

65. Why does Jeremiah command Baruch to repeat his words in the Temple? (Jer 36)

One of the things we learn as we grow older and more aware of our social surroundings is that there are clearly defined zones of power that can only be entered by certain people. For instance, only the high priest is allowed to enter the Holy of Holies in the Temple on the Day of Atonement (Lev 16:1–2). This stands in contrast to the open air scene in which Jeremiah delivered his Temple Sermon to a crowd standing in the street (Jer 7:2). When Jeremiah was unable to make another public appearance so soon after this spectacle, he sent his friend Baruch, a highly placed scribe and member of the bureaucracy, to present God's message predicting the coming destruction of Jerusalem by the Babylonians (36:29) in a more private setting. The prophet dictates his message to Baruch, who records it on a scroll. In so doing he elevates, at least in this instance, the importance of the scribe and the written word and diminishes that of the prophet and the oral presentation. Baruch first reads the prophet's message "in the hearing of all the people" inside the Temple, "in the chamber of Gemariah..., which was in the upper court, at the entry of the New Gate" (Jer 36:10). From this public place, which was accessible to a fairly large number of the male population, the scroll is then taken to the palace and read in a place set aside for a select group of the king's personal advisors, within "the secretary's chamber" (Jer 36:11–15). Finally, the scroll is read before the king and his officials "in his winter apartment," an area of the palace restricted to a very select group of the most powerful in the nation (Jer 36:21–22). Each of these locations represents the establishment of spheres of influence, defined by personal accessibility and proximity to increasingly powerful individuals. In the final setting, Jehoiakim is holding court within his palace. Around him would have been his chief advisors, petitioners, members of the royal family, and foreign dignitaries (36:21). It is before this audience that Jehoiakim makes his response to Jeremiah's message. He systematically cuts off the bottom of the scroll as it is drawn down and read. Each portion of the scroll is then thrown into a nearby brazier (36:23–25). In this graphic manner the king showed his unconcern and his total rejection of the prophet and his message. This bit of theater may have actually been directed at Jehoiakim's Babylonian master since it is quite likely that a Babylonian ambassador was in the room watching to see which master/God the king of Judah served. In any case, Jeremiah simply dictated the scroll once again and then cursed Jehoiakim and the royal house with extinction (36:30–32).

66. What enacted prophecies does Jeremiah use to visually present his message to the people of Jerusalem?

Jeremiah is particularly adept at employing street theater and props to illustrate his message of God's judgment on the city of Jerusalem. Among his theatrical performances is his presenting to the public an "unnatural lifestyle" (Jer 16:1–13; compare Ezek 24:15–27). He remains unmarried and childless and does not attend the funeral of his parents. In this way he demonstrates the imminent destruction that will befall the people and the futility of displaying normal human emotions of joy or sorrow when pestilence and famine await Judah's newborns (16:4) and the number of the dead will be so great that mourners will be too overwhelmed to even bury them (16:6). In another instance, the prophet enters the potters' district of Jerusalem to view a master potter at his wheel (Jer 18:1–11). This may well have been a common form of entertainment since the skill of these men would be well known and appreciated. Of course an audience may either make the potter nervous or too bold in his work and in this case the product was unsatisfactory and had to be reworked before he felt it was worthy of firing (18:4). This performance then serves as a means of declaring God's role as the divine potter, who shapes the destiny of the nations, for good or evil, depending upon his satisfaction with their willingness to "amend their ways" and turn from their own evil (18:5–11). Perhaps the most devastating of Jeremiah's public performances occurs when he processes through the city carrying a jar and accompanied by elders and priests and other spectators (Jer 19:1). Eventually, he comes to the Topheth in the Valley of Hinnom at the entrance to the Potsherd Gate (19:2). Here idolatrous rituals had taken place including the burning of children to the god Molech (2 Kgs 23:10), making it a perfect setting for the divine cursing of the city. In this shameful place, at God's direction, Jeremiah pronounces an execration curse upon Jerusalem for its idolatry and the shedding of innocent blood (19:4–5). Execration rituals were quite common in the ancient Near East, being used by governments to curse enemy nations and their leaders. It is the ultimate in public condemnation and in this case it is God cursing his own place of residence and its inhabitants to a grisly fate (19:7–9). The breaking of the jar enacts the curse and its scattered pieces represent a shattered covenant that cannot be mended (19:10–13). Of course, such a public act cannot be overlooked by the public officials. They have a vested interest in assuring the people that God would never allow his city or the temple that God has chosen "as a dwelling for his name" (Deut 12:11) to be destroyed. As a result, Pashur, the "chief officer in the house of the Lord," has Jeremiah arrested and placed in the stocks so that his message can be forgotten as the people concentrate on the prophet's humiliating posture and apparent helplessness (Jer 20:1–2). Once he is released, however, Jeremiah is quick to give Pashur a new name, "Terror-all-around," yet another form of enacted prophecy (compare the names of Hosea's children in Hos 1:4–9). The priest, who cared more about his own authority than the message of the Lord, will broadcast with this new name the coming terror of the exile that Babylon at God's command will inflict on Judah (Jer 20:4–6).

67. Why does Jeremiah write a letter to the exiles? (Jer 29:1–23)

When Nebuchadnezzar captured Jerusalem in 598 BCE he did not destroy the city. Instead, he took King Jehoiachin as his

prisoner, placed the king's uncle Zedekiah on the throne as a puppet ruler, and carried away a significant number of high ranking
individuals (priests, nobles, members of the royal family) to
Babylon as hostages (2 Kgs 24:12–17). Shortly after this humiliation took place, a number of prophetic voices were raised assuring the people that the exiles would be returned soon and that
Yahweh would take vengeance on the Babylonians (Jer 27:16).
Among the most prominent of these prophetic voices was
Hananiah, who declared in God's name that within two years the
sacred vessels of the temple, King Jehoiachin, and the exiles
would be returned and God would "break the yoke of the king of
Babylon" (Jer 28:2–4). Now, at that time, Jeremiah had been
parading through the streets of Jerusalem wearing a wooden ox
yoke to symbolize that the people should accept God's will for
them by bearing the yoke of Babylon as their penance. Hananiah
disputes this prophecy and physically breaks the yoke off of
Jeremiah's neck to demonstrate God's true intention of freeing the
people (Jer 28:10–11). This type of dispute is referred to as cognitive dissonance (see 1 Kgs 13:11–32; 22:13–28). Jeremiah himself seems puzzled and goes away for a time, but eventually
returns wearing an iron yoke to challenge Hananiah's statements
and to show that "the Lord has not sent you" (Jer 28:15), condemning him to death as a false prophet (see Deut 18:20–22).
Having weathered this storm, but realizing other false voices of
peace and hope were sure to be raised (29:8–9, 15, 30–32),
Jeremiah writes a letter to the people already in exile in Babylon
to indicate how they may survive the coming period of trial (Jer
29:1–23). This letter is remarkable in its recasting of how the
exiles are to worship Yahweh. First, they are to recognize that
they will remain in exile for generations (seventy years—29:10)
and therefore must settle into their new land, building houses for
themselves, starting businesses, and carrying on the everyday
activities of life including the arrangement of marriages for their
children (29:5–6). Most important, however, is the injunction to
pray for the prosperity of the city where they now dwell. They can

pray away from Jerusalem and the Temple. They can "seek me with all your heart" and be found by the Lord, and in their humility they will at last be gathered up and returned to their own land (29:7, 12–14). In this way, without the sacrificial rituals and an organized priesthood directing their religious life, they can concentrate on the relationship that had been the original basis of the covenantal agreement. They can survive as a displaced people and emerge intact from the predicament that their leaders have caused (29:21–23; see also 23:7–8).

68. What is the purpose of Jeremiah's "Book of Consolation"? (Jer 30–33)

During the long years of the exile it would have been easy for the people of Judah to become assimilated into the population and culture of Mesopotamia. It would have been obvious to many of them that Yahweh had been defeated and therefore they should look to the gods of Babylon for their protection and prosperity. For a faithful remnant to survive under these circumstances, Jeremiah had to present them with a theodicy of exile that justified the destruction of the nation's institutions and the transportation of its people into captivity (Jer 32:26–35). At the same time he needed to offer them the hope of eventual return and a future worth waiting for (32:36–44). In what has come to be called the "Book of Consolation," Jeremiah calmly reminds them that their "wound" is self-inflicted. They must recognize that no medicine can cure their illness of unfaithfulness. However, God will restore their health after they have been chastised in "just measure" (30:11–17). The prophet also uses language that incorporates and reverses some of his own prophetic imagery. Thus, in 30:8–9 he promises the people that God will "break the yoke" that binds them and restore them to their land under a Davidic ruler raised up for them by God's mercy (compare his call to accept this yoke in 27:12 and the promise of a "righteous Branch" to rule them in 23:5–6 and 33:15–16). To demonstrate that Yahweh is master of all events on earth, at the very moment of their glorious return, God will burst out in "a whirling tempest" to punish all the nations that have oppressed Judah (30:21–24). This will be a cause for celebration and dance as the cry goes out "Come, let us go up to Zion, to the Lord our God" (31:4–6; compare Pss 122 and 126). The land that had been desolated and emptied of its inhabitants shall be returned to life and a peaceful existence (33:10–13). On that day of restoration, God will write a new covenant on their hearts, one that they will experience as an abiding presence so that they truly "know the Lord" (31:31–34; 32:39–41; compare Hos 6:6). In this way Jeremiah instructs and consoles, offering them the chance to look into the mirror at their failures and to look forward to better days after the exile.

69. Why does Jeremiah "redeem" his relative's field in Anathoth? (Jer 32:1–25)

As is so often the case in the prophets (Isa 4:2; Hos 9:3; Joel 2:3), Jeremiah emphasizes the intrinsic importance of the land as part of God's covenant with the people. As Naboth tells Ahab when the king asked to purchase his subject's vineyard, the land is Israel's "ancestral inheritance," not something to be lightly sold or abandoned (1 Kgs 21:2–3). Thus, it is understandable that Jeremiah did not wish for a portion of his family's ancestral property to be sold out of their extended kinship group. When offered the opportunity to redeem it, Jeremiah quickly initiates the proper legal procedures, writing up multiple copies of the deed and having it signed by witnesses (Jer 32:6–12). Of course, at the time, Jeremiah was under house arrest and the city of Jerusalem was under siege by the Babylonian army (32:2). This does not sound like a propitious time to be worried about real estate transactions, especially in the light of Jeremiah's own prophecy that God intended to "give this city [and its king] into the hand of the king of Babylon" (32:3–5). What is happening here is therefore occurring on two levels. First it is the act of a dutiful kinsman, who accepts the responsibility placed on him by his family (compare the opposite response by the kinsman redeemer in Ruth 4:1–6). More importantly, however, Jeremiah is taking this opportunity to provide a public testimony to his prophecy of restoration. Although the deeds drawn up by Baruch are sealed away in jars for a long time, they will eventually be brought out as legal proof that with God's help "houses and fields and vineyards shall again be bought in this land" (Jer 32:14–15). The land sale also functions as a literary *inclusio* encompassing all of Israel's history from the time that Abraham purchased the Cave of Machpelah near Hebron as a burial plot (Gen 23:3–20). Abraham's witnessed deed provided the first legal proof of the covenant community's ownership of the Promised Land while Jeremiah's deed functions as the written reassurance that the land will remain in their possession.

EIGHT

EZEKIEL

70. What are the principal themes in the Book of Ezekiel?

Ezekiel functions as a prophet between 593 and 570 BCE. During that time he personally experiences the initial exile of the upper classes of Jerusalem, the period of growing tensions that lead up to the second siege of Jerusalem in 587 BCE, and the destruction of the city and the exile of an even larger segment of the population to Mesopotamia. As a result, his message can be divided between pre-587 and post-587 BCE pronouncements. Naturally, the prophetic themes he employs also differ because prior to the fall of Jerusalem he devotes all of his energies to a "doom and gloom" theodicy explaining why God will have "no pity" and will allow Jerusalem to be destroyed (Ezek 1–24; see Ezek 7:5–12). Then after the Temple is burned and the monarchy has come to an end, Ezekiel provides a series of oracles against foreign nations (Ezek 25–32) and a message of hope and restoration for the exiles that not only includes a return from exile but also the creation of a new covenant ("new heart and new spirit") and a detailed vision of the rebuilding of the Temple (Ezek 33–48). Ezekiel's prophetic performances do include some examples of street theater (Ezek 4–5), but the apocalyptic elements described in some of his visions (Ezek 38–39) and his recording of "out-of-body" experiences (Ezek 8–9), suggest that much of the material contained in his book represent personal rather than public reflections. To be sure, his primary aim, once he is released from the physical restraints placed on his message prior to the fall Jerusalem (Ezek 33:22), is to reassure his fellows exiles. Given the long period of exile, these reassurances may have actually taken the form of written oracles rather than spoken prophecies.

Pre-587 themes	• watchman theme (Ezek 3 and 33) • enacted prophecies of destruction (Ezek 4–5) • theodicy of defiled Temple (Ezek 8–10) • indictment of unfaithful wife (Ezek 16:1–58)
Post-587 themes	• individual responsibility vs. corporate identity (Ezek 14:12–14; 18; 33:10–20) • oracles against the nations (Ezek 25–32) • divine shepherd (Ezek 34) • apocalyptic images (Ezek 38–39) • restored nation (Ezek 36:16—37:14; 39:21–29) • restored Jerusalem Temple (Ezek 40–48)

71. How does Ezekiel's call narrative compare to those of other major prophets?

Although Ezekiel is an exact contemporary of Jeremiah, his call comes while he is a member of the exilic community around 593 BCE. He appears to have a high rank among them, sitting with the elders (Ezek 8:1), and he has an intimate knowledge of both the temple complex and the laws of purity that will later form the basis of the Holiness Code (Lev 17–26). This background places him on par with Isaiah as a priestly insider and in stark contrast to Jeremiah, the consummate outsider from Anathoth. Like earlier prophets, Ezekiel has a spectacular theophanic appearance that heralds his call from God. Amid the flashing storm clouds emerges a divine chariot drawn by multifaceted, winged creatures with four faces capable of transporting God "wherever the spirit would go" (1:4–14). The symbolism evokes images of God's omnipresence and the eye-filled rims of the chariot's wheels are suggestive of omnipotent sight (1:15–21). When God's presence was made known, seated on a throne, this apparition is intentionally indescribable, an indication that Ezekiel's intention is to remove as much of the anthropomorphic character of the divine as possible (1:26–28). This increases the mystery and the majesty of God's power evoking the familiar feeling of dread by the human who is being addressed (1:28b; compare 1 Kgs

19:11–13; Isa 6:5). Also like Jeremiah (Jer 1:7–9) and Moses (Exod 4:10–12), Ezekiel is reassured not to fear for he will have divine protection and will be given the words to speak (Ezek 2:6–7). Then, establishing a theme in Ezekiel's career of written testimony (see 24:2; 43:11), the newly appointed prophet is instructed to consume a scroll containing "words of lamentation and mourning and woe" (2:9–3:3). To complete his charge as God's messenger, Ezekiel is warned that although it is unlikely that his audience will choose to listen to his words (3:4–11), he must function as a watchman for their salvation (3:17). Their blood is literally on his head since without God's word of warning none would have the opportunity to repent and thereby survive the disaster that is to come (3:18–21). One additional point of comparison here is the repeated statements that God's spirit had entered the prophet (2:2; 3:24) and "the hand of the Lord" was upon Ezekiel (3:14, 22). These are reminiscent of the empowering of Elijah (1 Kgs 18:46) and Isaiah (8:11).

72. What is the meaning of Ezekiel's street theater prophecies in chapters 4–5?

One of the things that make enacted prophecies like those performed by Ezekiel in chapters 4 and 5 so powerful is that they present the prophet in out-of-character situations. As a priest, Ezekiel was required to strictly adhere to a set of regulations designed to maintain his ritual purity (see Lev 21). Yet in order to draw attention to his prophetic warning Ezekiel plays in the dirt using an inscribed clay brick and stick figures to portray the siege of Jerusalem (Ezek 4:1–3). His audience may conclude that he is mad, but they may also ask the question, "What does this mean for our future?" On another occasion the prophet is commanded to lie on his left side for 390 days, and then turn over and lie on his right side for 40 days, each day to represent the period of exile for the nations of Israel and Judah. Such prolonged inactivity would have caused him excruciating pain and horrible ulcers, and of course would have brought a crowd to his pallet every day. His suffering is then magnified when he is instructed to cook his starvation-diet meals over an "unclean fire" fueled with human dung (4:4–12). While he could face the pain inflicted on his person by his enforced position, Ezekiel gags at these cooking instructions and cannot force himself to consume impure food (see Exod 22:31; Lev 17:15). Only in this does God relent allowing him to cook on the more conventional animal dung fire, but warning the people through his actions that they must also consume a bitter meal in the coming days (4:15–17; 5:10). A third example of an enacted prophecy occurs when Ezekiel is told to use a sword blade to shave his head and beard (5:1–4). Again, this act functions as a way of drawing attention since a priest is prohibited from shaving his head or even the sides of his beard (Lev 21:5). Hair had great symbolic significance to the people of the ancient Near East. It was a part of their personal identity and for males represented adulthood and virility (see Hanu's shaming of David's ambassadors in 2 Sam 10:4). Similarly, prisoners of war were shaved to strip them of their former status (Isa 7:20). In addition, mourners shaved their heads as part of the cleansing process (Job 1:20) and to indicate to God their contrition (Jer 41:5). Ezekiel's action could have evoked any of these symbolic meanings, but when he divided the hair into three measured piles his audience would have seen that there was more. As he systematically attacked each pile, burning one, chopping another with a sword, and then scattering the third, they came to realize that he was once again portraying the suffering and death that would be visited on Jerusalem. As a pitiful aftermath, only the few hairs left embedded in his robe are seen to survive as the remnant of the people (5:2–4).

73. What are the "abominations" that Ezekiel sees in the Jerusalem Temple? (Ezek 8)

Just as Jeremiah listed the crimes of the people that were preventing God from being able to dwell in the temple (Jer 7:9–11),

Ezekiel describes a vision in which he is transported back to Jerusalem and given a guided tour of the many ways in which the temple of Yahweh had been defiled by foreign worship practices. At each stage of his journey, God warns him that "you will see still greater abominations" (8:6, 13, 15). From the moment when he is placed before the temple gate by his angelic guide, Ezekiel is scandalized at what has become of a place he knows so well. First, he is forced to seek an unorthodox entrance by tunneling through a wall because the entrance to the altar gate has been blocked by an "image of jealousy," a foreign idol (Ezek 8:5–8; see Exod 20:5). Finally inside, he is shocked to find himself in a hidden room whose walls are covered with portraits of the images of other gods (8:10). If this were not enough within the walls of God's sanctuary, the seventy elders of Judah are gathered there in secret to offer incense to these false gods for they fear that Yahweh has deserted them (8:11–12). The seventy elders had originally been commissioned by Moses to assist him in managing the people (Num 11:24–30). They also appear in company with Moses during the covenant renewal ceremony on Mt. Sinai (Exod 24:9) and would have been present among the elders gathered by King Solomon for the dedication of the Jerusalem Temple (1 Kgs 8:1). These individuals were supposed to represent the people; their demonstration of weakness and lack of faith must also represent these qualities among the general population. Urged on to witness even greater abominations, Ezekiel then sees blatant, public displays of worship for foreign deities. This includes a group of women in an outer court of the temple complex, who are "weeping for Tammuz," the Babylonian god believed to spend part of each year in the underworld as a representation of the change of seasons (8:14). It was believed that tears would cause the gods of the underworld to release him and thus to restore fertility to the earth. Of course, this was also a rejection of Yahweh's role of providing fertility as part of the covenant promise. In a similar show of devotion to the powers of an astral deity (see 2 Kgs 21:5; 23:11–12), a group of twenty-five men in the inner court bow down with their faces toward the sun in the east, literally turning their backs on God's altar (8:16). Such displays, probably related to the people's willingness to seek help for the city from all possible gods, deserve no forgiveness and God assures the prophet that their pleas will fall on deaf ears (8:18).

74. What is the significance of the six executioners and the scribe in Ezekiel 9?

One of the most powerful dramas in Israelite tradition is the story of the Tenth Plague in Egypt (Exod 12:1–13). Subsequent recitals and enactments of the Passover event made this an indelible memory for the people. Thus Ezekiel's use of elements from the story in his vision of the six executioners and the scribe would have had a chilling effect on his audience. This follows immediately after his vision of the abominations in the temple (Ezek 8) and is an appropriate response by God to the infidelity of the people of Jerusalem. Like the Levites who were ordered by Moses to go from one end of the Israelite encampment to the other and slay everyone who had bowed down to the golden calf (Exod 32:26–28), the seven men in Ezekiel's vision "go through the city," first marking the foreheads of the righteous who "groan over all the abominations," and then slay every person who does not have the mark (Ezek 9:4–7). The mark of righteousness serves the same purpose as the lamb's blood on the doorpost in Egypt (Exod 12:13). It sets these individuals aside, protecting them from harm, but also demonstrating once again that God is discriminating in his judgment and is always willing to spare those who show themselves to be righteous (see Noah in Gen 6:9–22). The use of a scribe in this vision also continues the theme of written prophecy established when Ezekiel was instructed to consume God's scroll (Ezek 3:1–3).

75. How does Ezekiel's "abandoned child" image compare with Hosea's marriage image? (Ezek 16)

Injunctions against adultery are found in Hammurabi's Code (## 129, 131, and 132), the Middle Assyrian Code (A.24), the Ten Commandments (Exod 20:14), and the Holiness Code (Lev 20:10), and is a source of scorn in biblical wisdom literature (Prov 6:32). Several of the prophets employ this heinous interpersonal crime as an analogy for Israel's violation of the covenant with Yahweh (Isa 57:3–13; Jer 3:9), but Hosea and Ezekiel make particularly effective use of the metaphor of the unfaithful wife. As noted above in responses 36 and 37, Hosea's marriage is equated with God's relationship with Israel and Gomer's harlotry is the equivalent of Israel's worship of other gods (Hosea 1–3). In that instance, Hosea first divorces his wife and then, like God, has mercy on her, offering to take her back if she will renounce her lovers/gods and pledge complete devotion to Hosea/God. Ezekiel includes the marriage metaphor in his story of the redeemed child, but there is no happy ending here. The tale begins with the tragedy of an abandoned female infant. Her family has had to make a difficult decision. Scarcity of food, the number and gender of other children, and potential costs of a dowry to the household may have factored into their decision, and in this case the newborn child is left in an open field still covered in its bloody afterbirth (Ezek 16:4–5). An abandoned child is left to the mercy of God and to any potential patron to adopt. Many must have died, but this one is lucky. She is adopted (the formula quoted here: "Live!" in v. 6), matures, and then marries her patron (the formula quoted here: "spread the edge of my cloak" in v. 8). The young woman is showered with all the gifts a husband can give: fine linen clothing, leather sandals, gold and silver jewelry, and choice foods to eat (16:10–14). However, in her vanity she used her fame and beauty to attract lovers, actually bribing them to serve her (16:33–34), and devoted her husband's gifts and even their children as sacrificial offerings to idols, forgetting who had once saved her life (16:15–22). Her "whorings" also include alliances with foreign powers (Egypt, v. 26; Assyria, v. 28; Chaldea, v. 29). For these crimes, God directs that this woman (= Judah) will be stripped naked by her lovers, stoned by a mob, pierced by swords, and have her houses burned down (16:35–41). She is then compared to her "sisters," Samaria and Sodom, and told that by comparison with her abominable acts they "appear righteous" (16:46–52). Not satisfied with physical and verbal punishment of his unfaithful wife, God chooses to forgive her, establishing an "everlasting covenant" with her as a final means of shaming and silencing her (16:59–63). This is not the tender and loving return to the proper married state described in Hosea 2:14–20. Things have gone too far by Ezekiel's time. Judah must be shamed and the choice is no longer theirs to return to God. Instead, like at the end of the flood that destroyed all humans except Noah and his family (Gen 8:1), God "remembers" (Ezek 16:60) and takes her back so she also will remember (16:61) what had once been and therefore will never dare to be unfaithful again.

76. What are the implications of the statement in Ezekiel 18:20, "The person who sins shall die"?

Some of the earliest legal traditions from ancient Israel include the principle of corporate identity. As expressed in Exodus 34:7, God declares that "the iniquity of the parents" will be visited "upon the children...to the third and fourth generation." Thus, the honor of a household must be upheld by all of its members and every member is affected by the actions of all others. If a father, as head of the household, is righteous and law-abiding (Job 1:1–5), then his entire household benefits from that honorable status (see Noah's family in Gen 6:9–7:1). Conversely, if the head of the household commits a crime, his household suffers with him (see the stoning of Achan and his family in Josh 7:20–26). Gradually, a shift took place in Israelite law allowing for more individual choice. For instance, in the Ten Commandments the four generations of punishment for offenders is mitigated for those who love God and keep the commandments (Exod 20:5). Even more straightforward is Deuteronomy 26:16 that declares that no one is to be executed for any crime that they have not personally committed. In Ezekiel's time, the shock associated with the fall of Jerusalem in 598 BCE and the deportation of some of the people brought out many questions about God's punishment of the nation and of those initially taken into exile. Had those who were taken been more sinful than those left behind (see the confiscation of their lands in Ezek 11:15)? Would the rest of the people face greater devastation because of these miscreants? To answer these questions and to assure the people that the community is neither lost nor left without the opportunity to make moral decisions, the prophet first points to King Zedekiah's violation of his oath to Nebuchadnezzar and Babylon. He declares that Zedekiah's decision will be punished by God with his removal from the throne and the defeat of his rebellious army (Ezek 17:12–21). That does not mean, however, that those who had had no part in Zedekiah's policies or had not violated God's law would also be punished. Thus "the children" (= exilic community) need not taste the bitterness imposed on their parents (= the king) any longer (18:1–3). Instead, since all human lives belong to God, the divine determination has now been made that "only the person who sins shall die" (18:4). None will have to pay for the sins of others (18:14–17, 20). This individual equation of exact reciprocity also allows for change. If the wicked repent their sins, they will be forgiven by God, who takes no "pleasure in the death of the wicked," preferring that they "turn away from their ways and live" (18:21–23; 33:11). In the same way, if the formerly righteous turn to crime, their former good deeds will not be remembered by God and they will face due punishment (18:24). It appears that Ezekiel expected a negative reaction to his message since he appended a divine rejoinder in response to those who charge that God's way is unfair (18:25–32). What the people do not seem to understand is that the household in Israelite society remains its chief social institution. There is no revocation of the laws that govern their behavior. The definitions of righteous and unrighteous persons in 18:5–13 are little more than a recital of the Ten Commandments. What has changed is the divine system of justice that now allows for a change in human behavior and does not burden an individual or a community with the weight of sin placed on his or her shoulders by kin or leaders.

77. Why does God promise to put a "new heart" and a "new spirit" into the people? (Ezek 36:26–28)

Part of Ezekiel's theodicy of exile is to explain to the people that for them to be truly purified by the experience and to come to a full appreciation of God's decision to maintain their covenant relationship despite their consistent failure to obey his words, they must receive a "new heart" and a "new spirit" from God (Ezek 18:31; 36:26–28). The word *heart* in this instance represents both the personal intellect of each member of the covenant community with which they will come to know God (Ps 27:8; Eccl 9:1; see Hos 6:6) as well as the former leadership of the nation. The old leadership or heart had failed them (see reference to Ahaz's "heart" = advisors in Isa 7:2) and now God must take charge as their divine shepherd (Ezek 34), bringing them back into the fold, and then placing over them a Davidic king, who will lead with the inspiration of God's spirit within him (34:23–24). For the sake of God's "holy name," Yahweh will gather the exiles from wherever they have been scattered to their own land, an act designed to show to all of the nations that "I am the Lord" (36:22–24). In the process, their "heart of stone" will be replaced with a heart of flesh, one that is more malleable and open to the change of attitude necessary for them to obey and fear God (Ezek 11:19; 36:26; compare Jer 32:39). Reiterating that this act of divine power is not for "your sake," the spirit of God is infused into their hearts transforming them into obedient servants who follow God's statutes and, most important, remember their former evil deeds and are ashamed (36:27–31). It is this ability to be ashamed that seems of greatest significance. In this envisioned world, the "stiff-necked" people (Exod 32:9; 2 Chr 30:8), who refused to listen or take action when warned by the prophets, will have passed away and a new, more perceptive people, who are worthy of the new covenant that God will establish with them, will take their place (36:19–20).

78. What is the significance of the Valley of Dry Bones in Ezekiel 37:1–14?

Whatever hopes remained for the miraculous survival of Jerusalem or a quick return from exile were dashed in 587 BCE when the Babylonian army systematically destroyed the city and deported a large portion of the remaining population of Judah to underpopulated areas in Mesopotamia. Ezekiel's vision of an old battlefield filled with the scattered, weathered bones of the fallen soldiers seems an apt metaphor for a people that many would consider to be expunged from the list of nations. It is possible to see this tightly woven visionary experience in Ezekiel 37:1–14 as a separate call narrative for Ezekiel, charging him with the eventual revival of the nation and its relocation to the Promised Land through the instrumentality of God's word and spirit (Hebrew: *rûaḥ*). However, it also functions as a reassurance to a despondent people (see the pathos in Ps 137) that they have not been abandoned by their God. In fact, what takes place in this vision is a creation story very similar to the one recounted in Genesis 2:7 in which God forms the first human from the dust and then animates him with the divine breath of life. In a similar fashion, Ezekiel is commanded to prophecy to the dusty bones he sees before him and they reform into whole bodies (37:4–8). However, they do not actually revive completely until Ezekiel is commanded to prophecy "to the breath" (37:9–10; compare Isa 42:5). Once this has been accomplished, the prophet is informed of the meaning of this resuscitation. He is charged with the prophetic mission to speak to the "whole house of Israel," a body that feels itself cut off and without hope. Through these words they will come to understand that it is possible for God to raise them from the grave of their exile and return them to their own land (37:11–12; 39:28–29). In doing this, God not only will prove once again to the people that "I am the Lord," but will also take the additional empowering step of reviving their faith by placing the divine "spirit within them." Given the opportunity to live again, the nation will recognize the power of the God who acts (36:27; 37:13–14).

79. Why does Ezekiel put so much effort into describing the rebuilding of the Temple? (Ezek 40–48)

Given his priestly background and his concerns for the ritual purity of the nation, it is not surprising to find a long exposition at the end of the Book of Ezekiel providing a detailed account of the rebuilding of Yahweh's Temple in Jerusalem. The climactic moment in Ezekiel's pre-587 BCE prophecies had been the departure of God's spirit and presence from the temple, abandoning that structure and the city to destruction (Ezek 10). Therefore, he would naturally see the full restoration of the people to full covenantal relationship with God in the reconstruction of the House of God and the return of God's spirit to that place (see Ezek 48:35—the renaming of the city to "The Lord Is There" [Yahweh Shammah]). The seed for this final section of Ezekiel is actually sown in chapter 20, which recites the history of the people's disobedience. At the critical moment when God is about to destroy them, the decision is reversed, "for the sake of his name" so that "it should not be profaned in the sight of the nations" (20:9, 14, 22). Ultimately, however, the exile became necessary and it served the purpose of purging from the nation its rebels and transgressors (20:38), who would not be returned to the land when the exile comes to an end. At that time, the faithful of Israel will serve God on his holy mountain (see 44:15–31 for restoration of the Zadokite priesthood). The "pleasing odor" of their offerings will be accepted (see Gen 8:21), and they will at last know "that I am the Lord" (20:41–44). Thus when Ezekiel is transported once more in visions to a high mountain in Israel, he is met by a divine guide who will conduct him through the holy structure that will once again serve as God's temple (40:2–4). Consistent with earlier visions, this guided tour of the new temple occurs at Yahweh's command and includes a return of God's glory to its precincts (Ezek 43:1–9) and an Eden-like character to the bounty it produces as the physical sign of the covenant (compare the waters flowing from below the threshold in 47:1–12 with the rivers flowing from Eden in Gen 2:10–14). God's return does not happen at the request of the people or because of any action that they have taken (compare Ezek 36:24–26 and 37:1–14). Since it commences in the twenty-fifth year of the exile (40:1), it occurs exactly one half of the way through a Jubilee period. The Jubilee requirement that all mortgaged property is to be return to its owners (Lev 25:8–13) fits very well with God's intention to return the exiles to their land and to their tribal portions (Ezek 47:13–48:14).

NINE

POSTEXILIC PROPHETS —
SIXTH CENTURY BCE

80. What are the principal themes in Second Isaiah? (chapters 40–55)

When it became clear that the Persian king Cyrus would soon complete his conquest of the Neo-Babylonian Empire ca. 540 BCE, the hopes of the exilic community were raised that they would soon be allowed to return home. Among the voices that heralded these events as a sign of God's power over the nations was a prophet or group of prophets who use some of the themes and language of—and even the name of—Isaiah. Referred to as Second Isaiah, these prophetic oracles from the end of the exilic period are found in chapters 40–55. The principal themes include: (1) the absurdity of idol worship and the revelation that there is no God but Yahweh (see 46:5–9); (2) a series of four Servant Songs forming a detailed theodicy of exile designed to show its value to Israel and to other nations (see 52:13–53:12); and (3) the use of Cyrus as an unknowing instrument of God's purpose (44:28–45:19). Distinguishing this section of the Book of Isaiah from chapters 1–39 (eighth century), the author(s) make it quite clear that they represent a different time period and a very different historical situation. They begin with a promise of healing and reconciliation: "Comfort, O Comfort my people...she has served her term...her penalty is paid" (40:2); "the Lord God comes with might...his reward is with him, and his recompense before him" (40:10). The unequaled divine act of releasing the exiles is proof of the majesty and incomparability of Yahweh. No idol or nation measures up to God: they are "less than nothing and emptiness" (40:17–20). The returned exiles will then provide a graphic demonstration to all peoples, "a light to the nations...causing kings and princes to prostrate themselves because of the Lord" (49:6–7). With those who choose to listen (51:4) and obey the call to return to Jerusalem, and because of God's "steadfast, sure love for David," the Lord will make an "everlasting covenant" so that they can serve as witnesses to the nations of God's glory (55:3–5). In this way, the historic event marking the end of the exile (last deeds) is equated with the Exodus from Egypt (first deeds), just as the "path in the Mighty Waters" is equated with the cosmic clearing of a path in the wilderness (41:3–4; 43:16–21).

81. Who is the "servant" spoken of in four poems in Second Isaiah?

The Servant Songs found within Second Isaiah are: (1) 42:1–4, Yahweh's chosen one, who will "bring forth justice to the nations"; (2) 49:1–6, formed in the womb by God (compare Jer 1:4–10) to "bring Jacob back to him" like Moses leading the Israelites in the wilderness, and to serve as a "light to the nations"; (3) 50:4–11, a servant who is submissive to the pain of exile, knowing "he who vindicates me is near"; and (4) 52:13–53:12, the "suffering servant," who "has borne our infirmities" and yet "out of his anguish he shall find satisfaction through knowledge." Because this material has gone through a long editorial process it is not possible to definitively affirm whether all of these songs were written by the same hand or are related. They all speak to the condition of the exile and the expectation that God will be vindicated through the release of his people. The identity of the "servant," however, remains an enigma. It is quite possible that the "servant" in some or all of these songs is a prophet who is calling the exiles to return to Jerusalem; or the exilic community as a whole, who have suffered through the shame of dislocation; or King Cyrus of Persia, whose political triumphs have served the purpose of Israel and their God. There is also the possibility that, in his desire to influence the exiles to return home, Second Isaiah has created a sectarian division, glorifying the suffering of those who support his call as the wise (compare Dan 11:33) and assuring them that they will one day "divide up the spoil with the strong" (Isa 53:12).

82. What is the significance of giving Cyrus the title of *anointed*?

By describing King Cyrus as "my shepherd" (Isa 44:28) and as the Lord's "anointed...whose right hand I have grasped" (45:1), this gives him the distinction of being the only foreign ruler to be granted titles that hitherto had been reserved for Israelite kings (1 Sam 12:3; 24:6) or the high priest (Lev 4:3). It is necessary to be careful not to confuse the use of the title *anointed* here with the messianic title found in apocalyptic writings (Dan 9:25; Zech 4:14) and in the New Testament (John 1:41; Acts 10:38). In Second Isaiah, Cyrus is a redeemer or savior figure, but he is not to take the place of a future Davidic ruler for the nation. His role is that of liberator under the direction, albeit unknown to him, of the God of Israel (45:5–6). There are obvious parallels between the language found in Isaiah 44:28–45:13 and Cyrus's own inscription, the Cyrus cylinder, which describes how the Babylonian god Marduk chose him to conquer Babylon. Whether there has been direct borrowing by Second Isaiah or whether the prophet simply made use of standard cultic speech, the most important point he makes is that Yahweh is the moving force behind Cyrus's victories and the source of the exiles' liberation.

Second Isaiah and the Cyrus Cylinder	
Yahweh chooses Cyrus ("grasps his hand," Isa 45:1a) to "subdue nations"	Marduk chooses Cyrus "to be king over all the world"
Yahweh opens doors and gates for Cyrus (45:1b–2)	Marduk made Cyrus enter his city, Babylon, without a fight or a battle
Yahweh calls Cyrus by his name (45:4)	Marduk calls out Cyrus's name
Cyrus's victory shows that Yahweh is Lord "from the rising of the sun and from the west" (45:6)	Marduk's patronage gives Cyrus rulership over all kings throughout the world
Yahweh "arouses" Cyrus to free the exiles (45:13; see Ezra 1:2–4; 6:3–5)	Cyrus returns the idols and the captive peoples to their lands

Context of Scripture, ed. Hallo and Younger, 2:124, pp. 315–16.

83. What are the principal themes in the Book of Haggai?

According to Ezra's account, God "stirred up the spirit of King Cyrus" (compare Isa 45:13) to issue a decree allowing the exiles to return to Jerusalem and rebuild the temple of Yahweh, "the God of heaven." In addition, the sacred vessels that Nebuchadnezzar had stripped from the Temple were restored (Ezra 1:2–4; 6:3–5; note Cyrus's Cylinder does earmark funds for the rebuilding of temples). An initial group of exiles returned to Jerusalem around 538 BCE with the Persian appointed governor Sheshbazzar (Ezra 5:16), and it is probable that additional groups continued to find their way back to the newly named province of Yehud over the next fifteen years. Among these returnees is another governor appointed by the Persians named Zerubbabel, who undertook the task of laying the foundation for the new Temple (Ezra 3:8–13). What then becomes clear in the tone of the Book of Haggai is that a delay in construction took place, possibly due to a lack of funds, the need to build houses and plant fields, and conflict with the people of the land who had not been taken away in the exile (Hag 1:2–6; Ezra 4:1–5). In a series of pronouncements made to Zerubbabel, Joshua, the chief priest, and to the "remnant of the people," Haggai steadfastly holds to a single theme pressuring them to complete the Temple (see Ezra 5:1–2). If they do not, then God will inflict a drought upon them and withhold the bounty of the land (Hag 7–11). The people's construction of houses for themselves and their toil to bring fields into cultivation, while not lifting a stone to rebuild God's House, are compared to a priest who makes a sacrificial offering while in an impure state (Hag 2:10–17). Neither is acceptable. Finally, the prophet attempts to overcome the political considerations that an appointed governor must deal with before he undertakes independent policies. Using a Davidic title, the "Signet Ring," Haggai assures Zerubbabel that God will "destroy the strength of the kingdoms of the nations," leaving him free to take up the mantle of the Davidic leadership and fulfill God's command (Hag 2:20–23). Again relying on Ezra, it appears that the Persian king

Darius, after a search of the royal archives, supplied additional funding and the work on the Temple was completed in 515 BCE (Ezra 6:1–15).

84. What are the principal themes in Zechariah 1–8?

An exact contemporary of Haggai (Ezra 5:1; Zech 1:1), Zechariah (chapters 1–8) also speaks during the early years of the reign of the Persian king Darius, when a change of royal administrator presents opportunities for additional funding and support (ca. 520–518 BCE). Zechariah's primary focus is also on the rebuilding of the Jerusalem Temple. Both of these prophets direct their message to the governor, Zerubbabel, and to Joshua, the high priest. Both contain themes centered on the proper restructuring of life and worship in the period of reconstruction immediately after the return from Babylonian exile. Where Zechariah differs is in the presentation of the majority of his message in eight visionary experiences (1:7–6:15). These interrelated visions portray the prophet's understanding of the universe as Yahweh's domain and within which are to be found the nations that rule the earth. The visions include an angelic guide and interpreter for the symbolic images portrayed to the prophet, a characteristic that will take full bloom in later apocalyptic literature (Dan 7–12; Zech 9–14). At the very center of his world lie Jerusalem, the Temple, and its leaders. The most important elements within these visions are the investiture scene in Zechariah 3:1–5 in which Joshua's filthy garments are transformed as a symbol of God's cleansing of the nation, and the vision of the two olive trees (Zech 4), which distinguishes the importance of Jerusalem's leaders, the "two anointed ones," to the complete restoration of the people's fortunes. Zechariah's use of the image of the "Branch" as a messianic title for Joshua (Zech 3:8), plays on the theme of a nation under an ideal Davidic ruler, who is guided in all things by Yahweh (compare Isa 4:2 and 11:1). The final portion of Zechariah includes a promise that Yahweh will return to Zion to dwell in majesty as Lord of hosts (Zech 8:1–3). Also contained here is an eschatological vision of an ingathering of all peoples to seek God's favor in Jerusalem (Zech 8:20–23).

85. What role does "the satan" play in Zechariah 3:1–2?

In his fourth visionary experience, Zechariah describes the high priest, Joshua, "standing before the angel of the Lord," confronted by "the *satan*" (God's prosecuting attorney) whose job is to accuse him of being unworthy to fill that position (Zech 3:1). Symbolic of his unfitness for this job are Joshua's filthy priestly robes (see description of priestly linen vestments in Ezek 44:17–18). They serve as a representation of the sins of the people and the priesthood as a whole. The exilic theme, that Yahweh's decision to restore Israel is not based on human actions or pleas, is seen here again when God orders that Joshua be given a new, clean set of clothes and a fresh turban (Zech 3:3–5; compare Isa 51:9–11; Ezek 36:22–32). This is followed by the familiar reassurance that obedience to the covenant will ensure God's blessings (see Deut 28:9; 1 Kgs 11:38) and will solidify both Joshua's place as high priest and the priestly community's role in administering the Temple and the courts (Zech 3:6–7). The role played by "the satan" in this symbolic drama is similar to that in Job 1:6–12 and 2:1–7. In both cases, this angelic being serves God while functioning as a catalyst for divine action or speech. The charge laid against Joshua provides the opportunity to rebuke the accusation as unjust and a rejection of God's decision to redeem the exiles. It also stands in contrast to the magnanimous gesture of God's angel, who orders a shift from "filthy clothes" to "festal apparent," marking the celebration due to one who at God's command has been cleansed of guilt (see Isa 43:25). An additional parallel is to be found in the shifting of Joseph's garments at the command of the pharaoh (Gen 41:41–45).

86. What are the principal themes in Third Isaiah? (chapters 56–66)

In the period between 538 and 500 BCE, the first waves of returning exiles were forced to scramble to establish themselves in the Jerusalem area. Much of their time had to be spent constructing homes, planting and harvesting fields, reestablishing commercial activity (Hag 1:4–6), and dealing with conflicts with the people who had remained on the land during the exile (Ezra 3:4–5) and Persian administrators (Tattenai and Shethar-bozenai— Ezra 5:3–4). When additional funds were finally supplied by the Persian emperor Darius, the temple was rebuilt and the priestly community resumed its role as officiants in the sacrificial cult and as judges on matters of ritual purity and religious practice (Ezra 3:1–6; 6:16–22). The third section of Isaiah (chapters 56–66) dates to this period of restoration and it functions as a voice that analyzes the postexilic community and asks whether it and Zion as God's holy mountain and dwelling place can be fully restored (see Isa 66:5–13, 20). The anonymous prophetic voice of Third Isaiah identifies itself in continuity with earlier prophets including Second Isaiah (see Isa 42:1), stating that "the spirit of the Lord God is upon me, because the Lord has anointed me...to bring good news to the oppressed...to proclaim liberty to the captives...to proclaim the year of the Lord's favor...to comfort all who mourn" (Isa 61:1–2). Like Second Isaiah, there is an emphasis on putting aside "former things" (Isa 43:18; 65:16–17) and instead looking toward an eventual fulfillment of those "new things" that are to come (Isa 42:9; 65:17; 66:22). The theme of a new age, attested to by the return of the exiles and the restoration of Zion (Isa 60), is a continuation of the prophecy in Isaiah 43:5–13, with Second Isaiah's "servant" being transformed in Third Isaiah into the righteous remnant that has returned to the land (60:21–22). However, the new age envisioned by Second Isaiah has been delayed because some of the social and cultic abuses that had been condemned in the past still plague the community. Thus, the social criticisms contained in Third Isaiah ("blind sentinels," shepherds without understanding, self-indulgent leaders—Isa 56:9–12) are echoes of First Isaiah's condemnation of hollow worship (Isa 1:12–15). The prophet provides a guide in dealing with this situation that will demonstrate once again what should be the true response of the faithful to God (Isa 58:1–14; compare Mic 6:4–6). Using fasting as his model of ineffectual worship, the prophet states that it is social justice, commitment to caring for the poor and homeless, and joyful attention to the Sabbath that will cause God to answer when they call for help (Isa 56:1–2; 58:6–9a).

87. Why does Third Isaiah place so much emphasis on Sabbath worship?

Sabbath had become increasingly important as an expression of Jewish identity during and after the exile. Failure to keep the strictures of Yahweh's day of rest (Exod 20:8–11) is seen as a serious violation of the covenant (see Ezek 22:6–12 and 23:37–39 for lists of crimes committed by the "princes of Israel"). During the tenure of Nehemiah's governorship in the fifth century BCE, he restricted all commerce on the Sabbath (Neh 10:31) and locked the gates of Jerusalem so no produce could be brought into the city for sale on that day (Neh 13:15–21). Sabbath observance is also included in the oath of obedience made by the Jerusalem community at Ezra's urging (Neh 10:28–39; see v. 31). All this suggests that Third Isaiah is focusing on a form of worship that already is considered to be a central feature of Jewish ritual practice. However, he takes Sabbath observance a step further by paralleling it with maintaining justice and refraining "from doing any evil" (Isa 56:1–2). Furthermore, he proclaims that no person, not even foreigners and eunuchs, should be excluded from entrance into the temple if they "keep the Sabbath…and hold fast my covenant" (56:3–6). This is echoed in Isaiah 58:1–12 in its exposition on proper worship versus hollow worship using fasting as the example. Third Isaiah maintains that the "fast" that God desires is to care for the weak and hungry, providing all persons with their rights under the law, and refraining from oppressing anyone (58:6–7). Those who refrain "from pursuing your own interests on my holy day" and take delight in the Sabbath will enjoy the benefits of the covenant promise (58:13–14). What may be at the heart of this extension of rights to Sabbath-keepers of all sorts is the clear separation that some within the Jerusalem community were making between "those of Israelite descent" and "all foreigners" and "the peoples of the lands" (Neh 9:2; 10:28). Third Isaiah provides a more inclusive vision of those who will be gathered to God's holy mountain to be joyful "in my house of prayer" (Isa 56:7).

TEN

POSTEXILIC PROPHETS—FIFTH CENTURY TO THIRD CENTURY BCE

88. What are the principal themes in the Book of Jonah?

Although the Book of Jonah is set during the period of Assyrian domination of Israel (eighth century BCE; see 2 Kgs 14:25 for the historical figure), its use of distinctive postexilic vocabulary, reliance on language contained in Jeremiah (18:7–8; 26:3; Jonah 3:9–10), and its use of traditional themes from the Psalms in Jonah's prayer (compare Ps 30 and Jonah 2) suggest a date of composition in the Second Temple period (post-515 BCE). The principal themes addressed in this short didactic story include: (1) Yahweh is the only true God (1:14–16; 3:5), the creator and force behind all of nature's elements (see Ps 104:5–23; Jonah 1:4, 17; 4:6–8); (2) those who repent their sins may expect God to hear their confession, may change his mind about punishing them, and will, when called upon, rescue them from adversity; (3) God is concerned with the welfare of all peoples of the earth (Jonah 4:2; universalism theme). The story also contains some comic elements playing on Jonah's attempt to flee God's call (1:3–17), the overwhelming response of the people of Nineveh that includes putting sackcloth on the animals (3:8), and Jonah's temper tantrum when God spares the city (4:1–8). Jonah's anger seems out of character with his prayer of thanksgiving in chapter 2. However, the prophet's petition parallels the abject response of the people and the king of Nineveh, who submit themselves to God's mercy based on Jonah's message of warning (3:4–9). Similarly, the scene in which the sailors entreat the sleeping Jonah to join them in praying for salvation from the storm (1:5–6) points to their greater sensitivity to God's power and this is echoed in the immediate response of the people of Nineveh to their peril.

89. Why is Jonah so reluctant to obey his call to be a prophet?

Jonah does not voice his objections aloud to God's call to "cry out against" Nineveh's wickedness (1:2–3). His reply comes in booking passage in the opposite direction, attempting to sail across the Mediterranean Sea to Tarshish in Spain and thus to escape the "presence of the Lord." A fuller explanation finally comes after Nineveh is spared and an angry Jonah grumbles, saying "Is not this what I said…why I fled to Tarshish…for I knew that you are a gracious God and merciful…and ready to relent from punishing" (4:2; compare Jer 26:19). In other words, Jonah wanted the Assyrians of Nineveh to be destroyed. It caused him so much frustration when God changes his mind and allows the city to survive, that he asks to die (compare Elijah in 1 Kgs 19:4, 8 and Job in Job 7:15–16). The reason is simple: the Assyrians were the most hated people of antiquity. They had conquered and pillaged all of the lands of the ancient Near East. In the process they destroyed much of the country of Israel and deported its people (2 Kgs 17:5–6, 24–28; 18:13). Many of the prophets had predicted that God would turn his terrible wrath on Assyria (Isa 10:12–19; Nah 2; Zeph 2:13–15), and yet Jonah's message has saved them. Of course, the historical reality is that Nineveh was destroyed in 612 BCE by a coalition of Medes and Babylonians. The use of Assyria in Jonah is the application of the "worst-case scenario" demonstrating that even these despised people are of concern to God and deserve the opportunity of being warned (see God's willingness to examine Sodom before destroying the city in Gen 18:20–32). This is therefore one of the best examples of the universalism theme (compare Rahab in Josh 2:8–21 and Na'aman in 2 Kgs 5:8–19).

90. What are the principal themes in the Book of Malachi?

Although the dating of this book is not certain, most scholars place it in the fifth century BCE during the Persian period. It is arranged in a series of six formal disputations, the first of which has God in conversation with Jacob/Israel (1:2–5) and then with the priests (1:6–2:9). In the final speech, God addresses an audience identified as "those who revere the Lord," whose response is simply to listen (3:13–4:3). Adherence to the covenant is the dominant theme in Malachi. A stark comparison is made between the offerings and actions of a corrupt priesthood (1:7–9, 12–14; 2:8) and the idealized true priest who recognizes the value of the covenant with Levi and "walks with me in integrity and uprightness" and provides "true instruction" to the people (2:4–7). The people of Judah are charged with violating the covenant through their mixed marriages (2:11), adultery, and divorce (2:14–16). Their wanton disregard for the law is manifested in the oppression of the workers, widows, and orphans (3:5; compare Deut 18:9–12; Ezek 22:7–12), and by robbing God of their tithes (3:8–9; see Neh 13:10–12). Throughout these discourses, God's universal power is cited as proof of his ability to bless and to punish his covenant partners (Mal 1:5, 11, 14; 2:10; 3:12; compare Deut 28:10). Even though sure and consistent punishment of evildoers is promised (Mal 2:1–3; 3:5–6), there is an element of hope as well for those who choose to be instructed (3:16–18). The epilogue in chapter 4 includes the "Day of Yahweh" theme (see Isa 22:12–14; Jer 4:9–10; Joel 2:1–2). Judgment comes on the wicked, but for the righteous this becomes a day of victory over their oppressors (Mal 4:1–3; compare Zech 10:5). A final admonition to obey the covenant of Moses is coupled with a promise to send Elijah (see 2 Kgs 2:11), restoring the prophetic voice that will "turn the hearts" of parents and children and thus prepare them for the day of the Lord's coming (Mal 4:4–5; compare Ezek 39:25–29).

91. Why is there such hatred of Edom in several of the prophetic books?

The popular theme in many of the prophets of condemning Esau/Edom for crimes perpetrated against Israel has its origins in the tradition of enmity between the twin brothers Esau and Jacob and Esau's eventual founding of the nation of Edom (Gen 25:19–34; 26:34; 27:1–41; 33:1–17). On a political level, the conflict may be based on long-standing border disputes (2 Chr 28:16) and the refusal of the Edomites to come to Jerusalem's aid in 587 BCE when the city was under siege by Nebuchadnezzar's army (see Ps 137:7; Lam 4:21). Rather than join the prophetic chorus condemning Edom, it should be noted that Judean refugees did find shelter in Edom after the destruction of Jerusalem (Jer 40:11). Thus additional reasons may need to be found for the citing of the fraternal conflict in the prophets (Isa 34:5–9; Jer 49:7–22; Obad 6, 18; Mal 1:2–3). To be sure, Edom's neutrality during Judah's fall saved them temporarily from being overrun themselves, but it created an additional source of tension between the nations that finds its expression in the series of oracles against enemy nations that center on the inevitability of God's vengeance upon them (Ezek 25:12–14). While there is no evidence of direct conflict between the Persian province of Yehud and Edom in the later Persian period, the continued control of the Negeb region by the "sons of Esau" = Idumeans (Obad 19–21; 1 Esdr 4:50) also may have contributed to the prophetic diatribes against this nation. In addition, it is important to the eschatological message of the later prophets that God's judgment on the nations prevents Edom from rebuilding itself. Instead the nations "beyond the borders of Israel" must be made to see the power of the Lord's anger and acknowledge who is the true God (Mal 1:2–5; compare Isa 43:8–13).

92. What are the principal themes in the Book of Joel?

Possibly a cultic figure of the Second Temple period in the fifth century BCE, the first portion of Joel's message follows a threefold pattern of locust plagues and droughts (1:2–4; 2:1–11), followed by a call to repentance and prayer (1:5–14; 2:12–17a), and a description of the prayer of lamentation (1:15–20; 2:17bc). Once the cycle is complete, the prayer is answered with God removing all dangers and calling on the "children of Zion" to rejoice in the restoration of the rains and a bountiful harvest (2:18–27; compare Isa 30:23–26). The final section of the book (2:28–3:21) consists of unrelated oracles containing familiar postexilic themes: (1) out-pouring of God's spirit (2:28–29; Ezek 39:29); (2) the restoration of Judah and Jerusalem's political fortunes with a judgment on all the nations (3:1–16, 19–21; Jer 51:24–58); and (3) an eschatological, Eden-like image of Judah (3:17–18; Zech 8:3–5). It is not possible to determine whether the locusts are simply a natural disaster for the small postexilic community that is interpreted here as a sign of God's displeasure (compare Hag 1:6–12) or whether they represent an invading army (see Nah 3:15). Since the solution prescribed by the prophet is abject repentance in sackcloth, fasting, and wailing before the altar (Joel 1:13–14; 2:12–13), this sounds like a call to restore the Temple and its priesthood to their proper function while there is still time to obtain God's mercy and freedom from addi-tional shame (2:14; 2:27).

93. What sort of day is the Day of Yahweh in Joel 2 and how does this compare to other prophets?

Amos is the first of the prophets to employ the "Day of the Lord" theme (5:18–20), but it must have existed prior to his time because he transforms what must have been an anticipation of God's favor into a dark day of judgment. This very gloomy image continues in the words of later prophets including Joel 2:1–2. What is envisioned is just punishment on a disobedient nation, using foreign powers and their armies to wreak havoc on them while making it clear that it is Yahweh who has brought this destruction on the people (see Isa 10:5). As long as the nations of Israel and Judah remained under threat by Assyria, Egypt, and Babylon, a theophany was necessary in order to demonstrate Yahweh's control over events (Lam 1:12–14). The prophets, of course, did not just call down God's wrath on their people. The Day of Yahweh is also a day of celebration when God restores a purified covenant community to its lands and turns his vengeance on the nations that had once been his instrument of punishment (Isa 11:10–16; Ezek 30:1–5).

Prophetic Use of "Day of the Lord" Theme	
Amos 5:18–20	"Alas for you who desire the day of the Lord?…It is darkness, not light."
Isaiah 13:6	"Wail, for the day of the Lord is near; it will come like destruction from the Almighty!"
Zephaniah 1:14–16	"The great day of the Lord is near.…a day of wrath…a day of ruin…a day of dark clouds and thick darkness"
Jeremiah 46:10	"That day is the day of the Lord God of hosts, a day of retribution, to gain vindication from his foes." (see Isa 34:8)
Ezekiel 30:3	"The day of the Lord is near…a time of doom for the nations"
Malachi 4:1–3	"The day is coming…when all the arrogant and all evildoers will be stubble"

94. What is apocalyptic literature?

Apocalyptic (based on the Greek *apokalypsis*) literature arose out of crisis, composed by people who were suffering oppression and persecution, and functions as an "unveiling" of events based on the direct intervention of God. This genre was intended to encourage perseverance by envisioning the destruction of the wicked and a glorious future for the faithful. Thus, Daniel was written to comfort the people of Judea who were suffering under the Seleucid ruler Antiochus Epiphanes (168–164 BCE). In their social, political, and economic alienation from the dominant community (whether it be the Seleucid Greeks or later the Romans), the apocalyptic writers constructed an alternate universe in which the downtrodden ultimately triumph. While much of apocalyptic literature is focused on the end-time and thus can be termed a form of eschatology, it should not be assumed that all eschatological literature is apocalyptic. Apocalyptic eschatology is more dependent on the supernatural and less on human action to achieve its goals. Thus in Daniel 7–12 God and his agents, the angels, reveal secrets of the future, a special knowledge possessed only by God, couched in bizarre imagery and number symbolism (strange beasts with multiple horns and wings in Dan 7:3–8). Of most importance is the eventual triumph of Yahweh over the kings, gods, and angel armies of enemy nations (see Dan 10:13–20; Zech 14:1–5). A way of differentiating apocalyptic literature from the collected oracles of the traditional prophets is that prophets wrote and spoke in their own names while an apocalypticist used the authority attached to the name of an ancient hero or prophet as their pseudonym. In addition, the sense of time is different between these two groups. Prophets believed God worked within history while an apocalypticist believed this world was intrinsically evil and that God's deliverance would have to come outside of history with a new creation. Prophecy, therefore, was an original and creative movement, less dependent on literary forms. Apocalyptic literature, however, uses the prophetic form in part and is less creative, depending instead on set literary forms.

Features of Apocalyptic Literature

Apocalyptic eschatology is a literary, not an oral, form.

Since Israel is incapable of fully realizing its covenant promise within the current reality of history and political domination, divine intervention is required (Dan 7:9–14).

Future events involving divine intervention are solely determined by God and are revealed to select prophets for them to record (Dan 9:20–27).

The revealed events are presented in visions employing symbolic images and language that must be interpreted by an angelic guide (Dan 8:15–27).

The oppressed people are assured that the current time of crisis will come to an end and the wicked will be punished (Zech 14:12–19), but secrecy must be maintained until that time (Dan 12:5–10).

Included in the eschatological vision of God's triumph is the inclusion of a last judgment, resurrection of the dead, and promises of an afterlife (Dan 12:2)

95. What are the principal themes in Zechariah 9–14?

Like the Book of Isaiah, Zechariah is divided into more than one section based on different time periods. The first section of Zechariah relates to the early postexilic period just prior to the construction of the temple in Jerusalem (ca. 520 BCE). The second section (chapters 9–14) comes from a later period, most likely the late fifth century, although no specific historical events can be ascribed to this material. Chapters 9–11 consist of several interconnected prophetic pronouncements, including the familiar oracles against the nations (Syria, Phoenicia, Philistia; Zech 9:1–8), which condemn specific cities in a geographic panorama in much the same way that Amos conducts his tour of nations to be punished (Amos 1:2–2:8; compare Ezek 25–30). There is also an emphasis on a coming ruler chosen by God to "command peace to all the nations" (9:9–10), although the triumphal entrance of the king (9:9) is set aside later when God expresses displeasure with the "shepherds," who have allowed the flock to suffer (10:2–3; compare Ezek 34:1–16) and required God to gather the scattered from among the nations (10:9–12). Chapter 11 continues this shepherding imagery to depict the dissolution of the nations of Israel and Judah and the disposal of their "worthless shepherds," who had caused such suffering to the sheep (11:7–17; 13:7–9). In the final section (chapter 12–14) of Zechariah, greater emphasis is placed on apocalyptic eschatological themes with a coming period of conflict in which Judah and

Jerusalem will experience both God-given victories over the besieging nations as well as great suffering (chapter 12). Chapter 13 focuses on false prophets, who claim by their speech and apparel to influence the people, while true prophets disavow any connection with the temple guilds or priestly establishment (13:2–6; compare Amos 7:14). A final eschatological vision appears in chapter 14, featuring a gathering of all nations against Jerusalem (14:1–2). Employing the Day of Yahweh theme, God's majesty is demonstrated in the battle and in cursing the enemy nations with plagues devastating humans and animals (14:4–15). God's victory will be marked by festivals that must also be attended by the nations or they will be cursed (14:16–19).

96. Is Daniel a prophet?

The Book of Daniel is divided into two sections: (1) a series of stories (chapters 1–6) about Daniel and his three friends (Shadrach, Meshach, and Abednego) set during the sixth century at the court of the Babylonian rulers Nebuchadnezzar, Belshazzar, and Darius the Mede; and (2) a series of apocalyptic eschatological visions (chapters 7–12) in which Daniel serves as a witness to these visions and the recorder of the interpretation provided to him by an angelic guide. In neither of these sections does Daniel act in the manner associated with the prophets, although he might be considered a diviner in his interpretation of dreams and in the deciphering of the "handwriting on the wall" (5:11–28). He has no call narrative and does not speak in the name of God. When he interprets dreams for king Nebuchadnezzar, he states that he has no special wisdom, but does this only so that the "interpretation may be known to the king," and thus the king must understand that the mysteries are revealed to him by the "God in heaven" (Dan 2:27–30). Of course, Daniel's ability to do this does distinguish him as a sage capable of "interpreting dreams, explaining riddles, and solving problems" (5:11–12). In those situations in which Daniel and his friends serve as role models of faith and obedience to the law (dietary laws in 1:8–17; idol worship in 3:1–26; and prayer in 6:7–24) they make no prophetic statements, but their miraculous survival impresses the king and gives them the opportunity to prosper (6:28). In the apocalyptic visions, Daniel is even less of an active participant. He receives dreams and visions, has them interpreted by angelic messengers, and writes them down, but they are to remain sealed "until the time of the end" (12:9). The actors on these visions are all angelic or divine, and Daniel is in no instance to speak of them to any human audience. Of course, his visions are read by the Jewish community, and their message of hope, coupled with an assurance that God would eventually remove their oppressors, carries out the intent of apocalyptic literature.

97. How does Daniel's ability to interpret dreams compare with Joseph's skills? (Gen 40–41; Dan 2:1–45; 4:18–27)

There are a number of similarities between the stories of Joseph and Daniel, and this is an indication that the Daniel narrative is dependent, at least in terms of its literary framework as a wisdom tale, on the Genesis account. In both narratives an Israelite (slave or exiled prisoner) operates within the context of a foreign royal court. In desperation, they each are asked to interpret dreams that the king's counselors, diviners, and magicians are incapable of understanding (Gen 41:1–13; Dan 2:16; 4:5–9). With the assistance of their God, both Joseph and Daniel are able to correctly answer the riddle of the dreams thereby demonstrating the power of Yahweh over all other gods (see Nebuchadnezzar's praise of God in Dan 4:34–37). In this way, both sets of stories fall within the framework of the theme of contest between gods (see the plague sequence in Exod 5–12 and Elijah's contest on Mt. Carmel in 1 Kgs 18). In addition to God's victory in these narratives, both Joseph and Daniel prosper as a result of their abilities, each rising to a position of authority at court and becoming a trusted advisor to the king from that point on (Gen 41:27–45; Dan

2:46–49; 4:18). In this way, both sets of episodes provide a model for the Israelites during a period of oppression, demonstrating that their God has not abandoned them and that they can rely on the Lord to care for and prosper them even within a foreign context.

98. How do the apocalyptic visions of strange beasts and cosmic battles relate to Israelite history? (Dan 7–12)

One of the most difficult tasks in reading the apocalyptic eschatological visions in Daniel 7–12 is to try to relate them in some way to actual events in Israelite history. Most likely written within the period between 168 and 164 BCE during the Maccabean Revolt against Seleucid control over Judea and Jerusalem, they provide reassurance that no foreign oppressor will be able to stand up to God's power when the deity decides to act. To demonstrate the truth of this assertion, the symbolic images contained in the first four visions are a recitation of past Israelite history. Each ultimately focuses on the inevitable demise of the current oppressor, the Seleucid ruler Antiochus Epiphanes IV, who had initiated a reform program designed to remove all vestiges of Jewish worship from the Jerusalem Temple and from the province of Judea and replace them with the worship of Greek deities (see 1 Macc 1:10–61). Thus Daniel is informed by his spirit guide (7:15–18) that the four beasts in his vision (Dan 7:3–8) represent former kingdoms that have dominated Israel in turn: Assyria, Babylonia, Persia/Media, and the current oppressor, the Seleucid Greeks. At God's command, each is judged with the earlier nations stripped of their dominion, and the four arrogant beasts executed (7:9–12). Since the fourth beast represents events in the time period of the author, more attention is given to its crimes and its punishment and humiliation are greater than all the rest (7:19–27). In the vision of the ram and the goat, as explained to Daniel by the angel Gabriel in Daniel 8, the Persian Empire is eclipsed by the victories of Alexander the Great and is divided among Alexander's generals (8:20–22). Antiochus in this vision is referred to as a king "skilled in intrigue," who will cause fearful destruction, but who will "be broken, and not by human hands" (8:23–25). Subsequent visions in this series supply information on the actual length of Israel's oppression (70 weeks = 7 x 70 years = 490 years), again finding completion in the reign of Antiochus (9:20–27) and cosmic conflicts between the angel armies of the nations of the earth (Dan 10–11). All this culminates in a final battle at the end of time in which the angel Michael defeats all of the nations (11:40–12:1). With this accomplished, a final judgment will take place, including the resurrection of the dead to face the judge (12:2). Still a period of discernment must continue until that day, and many of those who currently struggle may die before the end-time comes. Thus Daniel is told to seal up his book of visions until the time comes for the end of days (12:4, 9–12). The apocalyptic vision therefore works within the context of the events taking place in the second century BCE, providing encouragement to the leaders and supporters of the Maccabees, but pointing out that this will not be the end since that is to be determined by God, not by human agency.

99. Why does the idea of resurrection and last judgment suddenly appear in Daniel 12?

Throughout Israelite history there had been physical dangers to the people. Their small country had been invaded many times, their homes burned and robbed, and their neighbors taken away as slaves. In the historical context of the Book of Daniel, the period of the Maccabean Revolt of the mid-second century BCE, the oppressive policies of Antiochus IV (see 1 Macc 1:10–61; 2 Macc 6–7), and the lure of Hellenistic culture for many Jews (see 1 Macc 1:11–15; 2 Macc 4:10–15), some hope greater than eventual victory over enemies in this world was needed. It comes in the promise made in Daniel 12:2, 13, that "many of those who sleep in the dust of the earth shall awake, some to everlasting life, and some to shame and everlasting contempt." This is the first clearly articulated, explicit statement of a defined resurrection of at least "some" of the dead, a final judgment, and an afterlife in Jewish literature (compare Isa 25:6–8; 26:14–19; and the extended lifetimes following God's new creation in Isa 65:20–22). It, along with the description of the "three chasms" of the afterlife described in the pseudepigraphal work *1 Enoch* 24–26, has a great deal of influence on the further development of these concepts in some branches of Judaism (see *Psalms* of *Solomon* 3, 13–15; Josephus on Essenes and Pharisees in *Ant.* 18.1.3–5) and in the Christian movement (Matt 25:31–46; John 5:25–29; Acts 24:15). It is unclear why the author of Daniel chose to take this theological leap to advocate resurrection of the dead. It may be the result of a combination of factors, including the influence of Persian Zoroastrian beliefs in the afterlife and the thread of Israelite prophecy from the hopeful promise of a nation restored from the death of exile (Ezek 37:1–14) to the apocalyptic visions of Third Isaiah describing a blessed existence for God's chosen (Isa 65:17–25).

ELEVEN

FINAL THOUGHTS

100. Why did the tradition arise that prophecy ended after Ezra and Nehemiah (ca. 400 BCE)?

The canonical books of scripture contain no book of prophecy that is set in the time period after Ezra and Nehemiah. In this way a sense of completeness is provided to the promises of the canon and there are even very strong statements made warning the people against those who, in later times, attempt to portray themselves in their speech and their attire as prophets (Zech 13:4). What is interesting about this is that none of the prophets in the first section of the Book of the Twelve (Amos to Malachi), ranging from Amos to Zephaniah (representing the time period from the eighth to the sixth century and kings Uzziah/Jeroboam II to Josiah), are specifically referred to as prophets. Amos even denies that he is a prophet (i.e., a professional member of the cult associated with a temple or shrine; 7:14) but instead has become the transmitter of God's message without previous experience. There is also a great deal of confusion over who is a true prophet (as defined by Deut 18:18–22), which leads to some open conflicts among those who speak in the name of Yahweh (see Jeremiah vs. Hananiah in Jer 28). Only when we reach Haggai in the Persian period (1:1) is a person specifically referred to as "the prophet," and at that point any confusion over who truly speaks God's word is dispelled. Also from the Persian era, Zechariah is identified as a prophet (Zech 1:1; see Ezra 5:1), and, in developing his arguments to the postexilic community, he reiterates the words of what he calls the "former prophets" that the people of the past had refused to heed (Zech 7:7–12). The last of the prophets contained in the Book of the Twelve is Malachi. While he is not specifically referred to as a prophet, his message is addressed to the same postexilic community that is centered on the Second Temple in Jerusalem and deals with issues of proper ritual practice and social reform. He also points to the coming of a divine messenger of God (Mal 3:1–3), who is clearly a member of the divine assembly (see Isa 40:3–6), not a human prophet. The only prophet he exhorts the people to await is Elijah, the harbinger of the "great and terrible day of the Lord" (Mal 4:5). The case being made by these postexilic prophets is that the message of the "former prophets" continues to be valid and needs no further elaboration. From this point on no additional prophets are needed. Instead, the people are admonished to "return to me" and "I will return to you" (Zech 1:3). Thus Zechariah's visions (1:7–2:5; 3:1–6:8), each of which are interpreted for him by angelic messengers, restore a model of divine appearance that had been missing since the time of the ancestors (see Jacob's theophany at Bethel—Gen 28:10–17). Prophecy comes to an end and is replaced by divine messengers and divinely appointed servants (see Isaiah's Servant Songs in Isa 42–53).

101. Is there a resumption of the prophetic office with John the Baptist and Jesus?

There are several explicit references in the New Testament identifying John the Baptist as a prophet. The Gospels tie his appearance to the prophecy of a divine "messenger" in Isaiah 40:3 and include John's clothing and prophetic manner (Matt 3:4; Luke 1:6–8). Even clearer is the prophecy of John's "spirit-filled" father, Zechariah, who makes the statement that "you child will be called the prophet of the Most High" (Luke 1:76). Jesus also discusses the claim that John the Baptist is a prophet (Matt 11:7–15), but he carefully ties him to the prophet Elijah (Mark 9:11–13), whose reappearance is promised by Malachi as a sign of the "Day of the Lord" (Mal 4:5). In this way the question of the resumption of traditional prophecy is sidestepped in favor of a fulfillment of earlier prophecies and a heralding of the new age. Even more complex is the New Testament's attempt to combine the case for Jesus as the Messiah and the Son of God with several instances in which he is identified as a prophet. Thus, a direct reference to Jesus as a prophet comes in the story in which his miraculous powers and message are rejected by the people of his home village of Nazareth (Matt 13:54–58). In frustration, Jesus quotes what was probably a proverbial statement, "Prophets are not without honor except in their own country" (13:57; John 4:44). Another oblique reference to himself as a prophet is found in Jesus's prediction that "prophets, sages, and scribes" have been sent to the present generation, some of whom will be killed by the leaders of the community (Pharisees) so that a charge of shedding innocent blood can be laid upon them (Matt 23:34–36; Luke 11:45–52). On a grander scale, the pairing of Jesus with Moses and Elijah on the Mount of Transfiguration (Luke 9:28–36) powerfully ties him to prophetic tradition and provides a call narrative with Jesus identified as "my chosen" (compare "the servant" as God's "chosen" in Isa 42:1). The Gospels include many of Jesus's apocalyptic predictions regarding the advent of the kingdom of God on earth when all the forces of evil will be overthrown and the Son of man conducts a final judgment (Matt 13:40–43; Mark 8:38–9:1; Luke 21:34–36). After tying himself to the apocalyptic tradition with such statements (compare Zech 14:3–9), Jesus asks his disciples to relate what the people are saying about him. They respond that among the rumors is that he is "one of the ancient prophets" who had arisen. Jesus then counters this by asking who the disciples say he is and Peter responds, "The Messiah of God" (Luke 9:18–22).

SELECTED BIBLIOGRAPHY

General Reference

The Anchor Bible Dictionary. Edited by D. N. Freedman. New York: Doubleday, 1992.

Ancient Near Eastern Text. Edited by James Pritchard. Princeton, NJ: Princeton University Press, 1969.

The Cambridge Ancient History. Edited by J. Boardman et al. Cambridge: Cambridge University Press, 1970.

Civilizations of the Ancient Near East. Edited by Jack Sasson. New York: Scribners, 1995.

Context of Scripture. 3 vols. Edited by W. W. Hallo and K. L. Younger, Jr. Leiden: E. J. Brill, 1997–2002.

Dictionary of Biblical Imagery. Edited by L. Ryken et al. Downers Grove, IL: InterVarsity, 1998.

Dictionary of Deities and Demons in the Bible. Edited by K. van der Toorn et al. Leiden: E. J. Brill, 1995.

The New Encyclopedia of Archaeological Excavations in the Holy Land. Edited by E. Stern. New York: Simon & Schuster, 1993.

Old Testament Parallels: Laws and Stories from the Ancient Near East. Revised and expanded 3rd ed. Victor H. Matthews and Don C. Benjamin. New York/Mahwah, NJ: Paulist Press, 2007.

The Oxford Encyclopedia of Archaeology in the Near East. Edited by E. Meyers. New York: Oxford University Press, 1997.

Books on Particular Aspects of Biblical Background

Beitzel, B. *The Moody Atlas of Bible Lands*. Chicago: Moody, 1985.

Berquist, J. *Judaism in Persia's Shadow*. Minneapolis: Fortress, 1995.

Blenkinsopp, J. *Sage, Priest, Prophet: Religious and Intellectual Leadership in Ancient Israel*. Louisville: Westminster John Knox, 1995.

Borowski, O. *Agriculture in Iron Age Israel*. Winona Lake, IN: Eisenbrauns, 1987.

————. *Every Living Thing*. Walnut Creek, CA: Alta Mira, 1998.

Bottéro, J. *Mesopotamia*. Chicago: University of Chicago Press, 1992.

Cook, S. L. *Prophecy and Apocalypticism: The Postexilic Social Setting*. Minneapolis: Fortress, 1995.

Cross, F. M. *Canaanite Myth and Hebrew Epic*. Cambridge: Harvard University Press, 1971.

Cryer, F. H. *Divination in Ancient Israel and Its Near Eastern Environment*. Sheffield: JSOT Press, 1994.

Davies, W. D. et al. *The Cambridge History of Judaism*. Vol. 1, *The Persian Period*. Cambridge: Cambridge University Press, 1984.

Dearman, A. *Religion and Culture in Ancient Israel*. Peabody, MA: Hendrickson, 1992.

Dempsey, C. J. *The Prophets: A Liberation-Critical Reading*. Minneapolis: Fortress, 2000.

Eskenazi, T., and K. Richards, eds. *Second Temple Studies*. Sheffield: JSOT Press, 1994.

Gershevitch, I., ed. *The Cambridge History of Iran*. Vol. 2, *The Median and Achaemenid Periods*. Cambridge: Cambridge University Press, 1985.

Gowan, D. E. *Theology of the Prophetic Books: The Death and Resurrection of Israel*. Louisville: Westminster John Knox, 1998.

Grabbe, L. *Judaism from Cyrus to Hadrian*. Minneapolis: Fortress, 1992.

————. *Priests, Prophets, Diviners, Sages: A Socio-Historical Study of Religious Specialists in Ancient Israel*. Valley Forge, PA: Trinity International, 1995.

Hoerth, A., G. Mattingly, and E. Yamauchi. *Peoples of the Old Testament World*. Grand Rapids: Baker, 1994.

Horowitz, W. *Mesopotamian Cosmic Geography*. Winona Lake: Eisenbrauns, 1998.

Jacobsen, T. *The Harps That Once...* New Haven, CT: Yale University Press, 1987.

————. *Treasures of Darkness*. New Haven, CT: Yale University Press, 1976.

Keel, O. *The Symbolism of the Biblical World*. New York: Seabury, 1978.

Keel, O., and C. Uehlinger. *Gods, Goddesses and Images of God in Ancient Israel*. Minneapolis: Fortress, 1998.

King, P. *Amos, Hosea, Micah: An Archaeological Commentary*. Philadelphia: Westminster, 1988.

Kuhrt, A. *The Ancient Near East, 3000–330 BC*. London: Routledge, 1997.

Lambert, W. G. *Babylonian Wisdom Literature*. Oxford: Clarendon Press, 1960.

Lichtheim, Miriam. *Ancient Egyptian Literature*. Berkeley: University of California Press, 1980.

Matthews, V. H. *Manners and Customs in the Bible*. 3rd ed. Peabody, MA: Hendrickson, 2006.

Matthews, V. H., and D. C. Benjamin. *The Social World of Ancient Israel*. Peabody, MA: Hendrickson, 1993.

Mazar, Amihai. *Archaeology of the Land of the Bible*. New York: Doubleday, 1990.

Miller, J. M., and J. Hayes. *A History of Ancient Israel and Judah.* Philadelphia: Westminster, 1986.

Nemet-Nejat, Karen Rhea. *Daily Life in Ancient Mesopotamia.* Westport, CT: Greenwood, 1998.

Overholt, T. W. *Channels of Prophecy: The Social Dynamics of Prophetic Activity.* Minneapolis: Fortress, 1989.

Peckham, B. *History and Prophecy: The Development of Late Judean Literary Traditions.* New York: Doubleday, 1993.

Pleins, J. D. *The Social Visions of the Hebrew Bible.* Louisville: Westminster John Knox, 2001.

Rasmussen, Carl. *NIV Atlas of the Bible.* Grand Rapids: Zondervan, 1989.

Redford, D. B. *Egypt, Canaan, and Israel in Ancient Times.* Princeton, NJ: Princeton University Press, 1992.

Reiner, E. *Astral Magic in Babylonia.* Philadelphia: American Philosophical Society, 1995.

Roaf, M. *Cultural Atlas of Mesopotamia and the Ancient Near East.* New York: Facts on File, 1990.

Saggs, H. W. F. *Encounter with the Divine in Mesopotamia and Israel.* London: Athlone, 1978.

———. *The Greatness That Was Babylon.* New York: Mentor, 1962.

———. *The Might That Was Assyria.* London: Sidgwick & Jackson, 1984.

Snell, D. *Life in the Ancient Near East.* New Haven, CT: Yale University Press, 1997.

Toorn, K. van der. *Sin and Sanction in Israel and Mesopotamia.* Assen: Van Gorcum, 1985.

Weinfeld, M. *Social Justice in Ancient Israel.* Minneapolis: Fortress, 1995.

Wiseman, D. J. *Nebuchadrezzar and Babylon.* New York: Oxford University Press, 1985.

Wright, C. J. H. *God's People in God's Land.* Grand Rapids: Eerdmans, 1990.

Yamauchi, E. *Persia and the Bible.* Grand Rapids: Baker, 1990.

Commentaries

Isaiah

Oswalt, J. *The Book of Isaiah*. 2 vols. Grand Rapids: Eerdmans, 1986, 1997.

Watts, J. D. W. *Isaiah 1–33*. Waco: Word, 1985.

————. *Isaiah 34–66*. Waco: Word, 1987.

Wildberger, H. *Isaiah 1–12*. Minneapolis: Fortress, 1991.

————. *Isaiah 13–27*. Minneapolis: Fortress, 1998.

Jeremiah

Holladay, W. *Jeremiah 1*. Minneapolis: Fortress, 1986.

————. *Jeremiah 2*. Minneapolis: Fortress, 1989.

Keown, G. L., P. J. Scalise, and T. G. Smothers. *Jeremiah 26–52*. Dallas: Word, 1995.

Thompson, J. A. *The Book of Jeremiah*. Grand Rapids: Eerdmans, 1980.

Ezekiel

Allen, L. *Ezekiel*. 2 vols. Dallas: Word, 1990, 1994.

Block, D. I. *The Book of Ezekiel*. 2 vols. Grand Rapids: Eerdmans, 1997, 1998.

Bodi, D. *The Book of Ezekiel and the Poem of Erra*. Freiburg, Schweiz: Vandenhoeck & Ruprecht, 1991.

Greenberg, M. *Ezekiel 1–20*. New York: Doubleday, 1983.

————. *Ezekiel 21–37*. New York: Doubleday, 1997.

Zimmerli, W. *Ezekiel 1*. Minneapolis: Fortress, 1979.

————. *Ezekiel 2*. Minneapolis: Fortress, 1983.

Daniel

Baldwin, J. *Daniel*. Downers Grove, IL: InterVarsity, 1978.
Collins, J. J. *Daniel*. Minneapolis: Fortress, 1993.
Goldingay, J. *Daniel*. Dallas: Word, 1989.

Hosea

Andersen, F. I., and D. N. Freedman. *Hosea*. New York: Doubleday, 1980.
MacIntosh, A. A. *A Critical and Exegetical Commentary on Hosea*. Edinburgh: T&T Clark, 1997.
Stuart, D. *Hosea-Jonah*. Dallas: Word, 1987.
Wolff, H. W. *A Commentary on the Book of the Prophet Hosea*. Minneapolis: Fortress, 1974.

Joel

Allen, L. C. *The Books of Joel, Obadiah, Jonah, and Micah*. Grand Rapids: Eerdmans, 1976.
Crenshaw, J. *Joel*. New York: Doubleday, 1995.
Hubbard, D. *Joel, Amos*. Downers Grove, IL: InterVarsity, 1989.
Stuart, D. *Hosea-Jonah*. Dallas: Word, 1987.
Wolff, H. W. *Joel and Amos*. Minneapolis: Fortress, 1977.

Amos

Andersen, F., and D. N. Freedman. *Amos*. New York: Doubleday, 1989.
Jeremias, J. *The Book of Amos*. Louisville: Westminster John Knox, 1998.
Paul, S. *A Commentary on the Book of Amos*. Minneapolis: Fortress, 1991.
Wolff, H. W. *A Commentary on the Books of the Prophets Joel and Amos*. Minneapolis: Fortress, 1977.

Obadiah

Allen, L. C. *The Books of Joel, Obadiah, Jonah, and Micah.* Grand Rapids: Eerdmans, 1976.
Raabe, P. R. *Obadiah.* New York: Doubleday, 1996.
Wolff, H. W. *Obadiah and Jonah.* Minneapolis: Fortress, 1986.

Jonah

Limburg, J. *Jonah.* Louisville: Westminster John Knox, 1993.
Sasson, Jack. *Jonah.* New York: Doubleday, 1990.
Walton, John. *Jonah.* Grand Rapids: Zondervan, 1982.
Wolff, H. W. *Obadiah and Jonah.* Minneapolis: Fortress, 1986.

Micah

Ben Zvi, E. *Micah.* Grand Rapids: Eerdmans, 2000.
Hillers, D. *Micah.* Minneapolis: Fortress, 1983.
Mays, J. M. *Micah.* Philadelphia: Westminster, 1976.

Nahum

Baker, D. *Nahum, Habakkuk, Zephaniah.* Downers Grove, IL: InterVarsity, 1988.
Roberts, J. J. M. *Nahum, Habakkuk, and Zephaniah: a Commentary.* Louisville: Westminster John Knox, 1991.

Habakkuk

Roberts, J. J. M. *Nahum, Habakkuk, and Zephaniah: A Commentary.* Louisville: Westminster John Knox, 1991.
Smith, R. L. *Micah-Malachi.* Waco: Word, 1984.

Zephaniah

Berlin, A. *Zephaniah*. New York: Doubleday, 1994.
Roberts, J. J. M. *Nahum, Habakkuk, and Zephaniah: A Commentary*. Louisville: Westminster John Knox, 1991.
Smith, R. L. *Micah-Malachi*. Waco: Word, 1984.

Haggai

Meyers, E., and C. Meyers. *Haggai, Zechariah 1–8*. New York: Doubleday, 1987.
Verhoef, P. A. *The Books of Haggai and Malachi*. Grand Rapids: Eerdmans, 1986.
Wolff, H. W. *Haggai*. Minneapolis: Fortress, 1988.

Zechariah

Ellis, R. S. *Foundation Deposits in Ancient Mesopotamia*. New Haven, CT: Yale University Press, 1968.
Halpern, B. "The Ritual Background of Zechariah's Temple Song." *Catholic Biblical Quarterly* 40 (1978): 167–90.
Meyers, E., and C. Meyers. *Zechariah 9–14*. New York: Doubleday, 1993.

Malachi

Glazier-McDonald, B. *The Divine Messenger*. Atlanta: Scholars, 1987.
Hill, A. *Malachi*. New York: Doubleday, 1998.
Petersen, D. L. *Zechariah 9–14 and Malachi*. Louisville: Westminster John Knox, 1995.